braque

braque

Lara Vinca Masini

Hamlyn
London   New York   Sydney   Toronto

twentieth–century masters
General editors: H. L. Jaffé and A. Busignani

© Copyright in the text Sadea/Sansoni, Florence 1969
© Copyright in the pictures ADAGP, Paris 1969
© Copyright this edition The Hamlyn Publishing Group Limited 1971
London · New York · Sydney · Toronto
Hamlyn House, Feltham, Middlesex, England
ISBN 0 600 31206 2

Colour lithography: Zincotipia Moderna, Florence
Printing and binding: Cox and Wyman Limited
London, Fakenham and Reading

Distributed in the United States of America by Crown Publishers Inc.

contents

List of colour illustrations

List of black-and-white illustrations

Braque the master

'I would find it difficult to choose between Braque as the most inventive artist of our time and Braque as the most versatile master. However, if a great painter is one who gives the most heightened and fertile significance to painting, then I would choose Braque as a master without hesitation.'

This judgement, that of Jean Paulhan, still holds; from it he derived the title of his famous book *Braque the Master,* published by Gallimard in 1952, written between 1940 and 1952, first appearing, incomplete, under No. 40 of *Poésies.* Braque is a painter on whom critical judgement has not fundamentally altered. For though the development of his painting was marked by frequent and considerable changes, these occurred not in terms of a trajectory purely within the realised works but rather in terms of his approach towards pictorial method.

A brief series of quotations taken from various critical texts, dating from the twenty years following the birth of Cubism, are enough to demonstrate the fundamental coincidence of opinion on Braque's work, which has been generally confirmed in later writings.

From Guillaume Apollinaire's Preface to the catalogue of Braque's exhibition at the Galerie Kahnweiler (9th–28th November, 1908): 'Here is Georges Braque. He leads an admirable life. He passionately struggles to attain beauty and does so, one might say, without effort. His compositions contain the harmony and completion which have been long awaited . . . Their beauty is tender and the mother-of-pearl of his pictures endows our intellect with iridescence . . . This painter is angelic. Purer than other mortals, he is not preoccupied with the world outside his art which would otherwise entail his descent from the paradise he inhabits.'

Ardengo Soffici: 'Certainly he lacks the versatility which makes Picasso the living compendium of ten years of pictorial research; but, compensated by love, sharpness and delicacy, especially in the more recent pictures . . . Braque with his slightly less rigorous technique obtains a form of musical calm filled with both gentleness and severity.'[1]

E. Bove: 'In each canvas of this great painter there exists an integrity which does not deceive. His dominant qualities are maturity and strength. The Profane; confronted by this work is immediately overpowered by equilibrium, security, confidence. Nothing is left to chance. All is firm, slow, strong . . . his painting is the emanation of his soul . . . through him a new notion of painting is being born, more serious and more austere.'[2]

1 A. Soffici, *Cubismo e oltre,* Florence, 1913.
2 E. Bove, 'Georges Braque' in *Formes,* No. 3, Paris, March 1930.

1 *Portrait de Mme Johanet*
1900–1, oil on canvas
24 × 19½ in (61 × 50 cm)
Galerie Maeght, Paris

Controversy of Cubism

It is not the critical opinion of Braque as an artist which varies, but rather the judgement of one of the most important movements of twentieth-century art, Cubism, of which Braque was a fundamental protagonist, if not the principal exponent.

However, the changing critical assessment of Cubism impinges on Braque's work, which itself can be located in the light of such an appreciation. The changing view of Cubism is therefore relevant.

In a recent study of Cubism, still in the course of being published, I have tried to show how it was a reactionary movement. This does not mean, however, that in the wake of scientific discoveries and philosophical developments, the Cubists intended to destroy traditional pictorial vision, replacing it by the fourth dimension and the space-time factor, implicit in the process of 'simultaneous vision'. Rather, they restored the intellectual dimension within the pictorial vision itself.

Cubism, therefore, represented innovation within the tradition of classical figurative painting. Its object was not to overthrow it; rather, it represented a further and ultimate stage of development, still posed in terms of 'form'. However, form was no longer understood as 'transcendence' but as 'absolute immanence', as a 'formal experience' (Argan). Thus the problem was altered and transposed, not overthrown and reposed anew.

Cubist painting tried to resolve the problem of space and volume through the space-time dimension of the 'continuous present', reducing them to planes and compact surfaces. Cubist method was opposed to three-dimensional or volumetric representation. The movement thus carried the possibilities of traditional perspective to their extreme limits at the same time it

provided the means to carry out a complete revision and reinterpretation of past art-forms. It was certainly not a revolutionary movement, particularly because it did not presuppose a political choice on the part of its exponents.

It was revolutionary only in terms of its method, based on research and continuous experiment, in other words, in the way it conceived the work of the artist in ethical terms. Here lies the distinction between 'contemporary' and 'modern' art. More recently this artistic emphasis has itself been put in question.

It is precisely this aspect of Cubism which is not represented by Picasso, the other central artist of the movement, but rather by Braque.

Argan writes: 'The artist must make a political choice, and he does so at the very moment he chooses to devote himself to an activity which can only attain its full value in a classless society. At least three of the major artists of the century (not to mention the architects), made this choice with a spirit of audacity which reminds one of the religious reformers of the sixteenth century: Kandinsky, Klee, Mondrian . . . they renounced without regret the joy of inventiveness for the struggles of research. Undoubtedly, the immense prestige of Picasso could have determined the fate of the new poetic language. But Picasso did not become a Calvinist; he remained Catholic, perhaps not to renounce the joys of blasphemy. His arrogant response was: 'I do not seek, I find' – the most famous, but morally the worst, statement he ever made.[3]

Perhaps we owe to Picasso the fact that Cubism was not a revolutionary

2 *La Côte de Grace à Houffleur*
1905, oil on canvas
$19\frac{1}{2} \times 23\frac{1}{2}$ in (50 × 60 cm)
Le Havre Museum

3 G. C. Argan in the introduction to *Picasso* by R. Penrose, Turin, 1969.

3 *Paysage à la Ciotat*
1907, oil on canvas
15 × 18 in (38 × 46 cm)
Private collection, Pittsburgh

movement, but rather a movement of revision. He took what he found and transformed everything, consumed all in a devouring fire, from which arose the phoenix of his indefatigable fantasy, his 'genius'. To speak of genius in the case of Picasso places him within the orbit of traditional culture, interpreting him, as Argan points out, as a classical artist.[4] Braque, on the other hand, represents, after Cézanne, the last meeting point between the great French tradition and modern art; he is not 'classical' in the same sense as Picasso. He placed experiment and research at the heart of his work. It is to him that we owe the revolutionary aspect of Cubism. For Braque, Picasso's famous statement would have to be read backwards. Nothing for him is simply found by accident or unexpected inspiration. Every discovery is a result of a research, and passes through the subtle filter of a continuous, tireless process of verification. The fire of his fervour ('I do not seek exaltation; fervour is enough for me') is not devouring but purifying; it liberates the artistic object from all the pseudo-cultural and literary appendages that weigh it down. However, this liberation of art for its own autonomous development, freed from any impediments (as regards content, means, and linguistic conditions), remained for Braque, none the less, tied to the traditional concept of painting.

In this way we can also trace the two aspects of Cubism in Braque's creative work; on the one hand a non-revolutionary review within the linguistic terms of painting, and on the other, its *avant-garde* character, its definition of artistic work as open experimentation, its rejection of the masterpiece and the monument.

In the first sense, he was the last of the great painters of the 'classical' French tradition with all the characteristics that contemporary artistic culture has by now rejected: 'pure' painting, based on colour and naturalism (though his naturalism must be understood in its own right), the representation of the real and the mental incapacity to conceive of the picture other than in its own terms.

However, at the same time, we owe to him some of the fundamental discoveries which have decisively orientated the development of contemporary art. These discoveries were: the definition of the picture in terms of space; the conception of it as an object; the insertion of newsprint, letters, numbers and signs which serve as 'real' forms, existing only by virtue of the

4 G. C. Argan *op. cit.*

10

painting. These 'concrete forms . . . existed outside three-dimensional space; their insertion in the picture created a distinction between objects situated in space and objects which did not belong to space'; hence the *papier collé,* employed by Braque also for an evocative, poetic purpose.

This does not mean that Braque's importance as a painter can be limited to the sphere of Cubism. On the contrary, though his Cubist experience was more arduous, perhaps more intense, Braque succeeded even more than Picasso in surpassing Cubism in the subsequent development of his work, not through drastic changes, but rather by way of subtle variations, modulations and transpositions.

'A painting which does not disturb? Can such a thing exist?' This is almost a motto, a programmatic declaration, like the famous triad: 'impregnation, obsession, hallucination', a sort of progression with which Braque defined his work and explained his approach to painting. *Hallucination* is the result of a long *impregnation,* of a continuous, *obsessive,* lucid process of rethinking.

It is according to this pre-established procedure, conscientiously worked out in practice, that we can follow the process of realisation of Braque's unique *œuvre,* and the evolution of his language from his youth onwards.

Reserved in character and quite the opposite to an exhibitionist, Braque

Impregnation, obsession, hallucination

4 *Grand Nu*
1907–8, signed at bottom right
oil on canvas
57 × 40 in (145·5 × 101·5 cm)
Madame Cuttoli collection, Paris

5 *Etude de Nu*
1908, etching, 1953 print
11 × 7½ in (28 × 19·5 cm)
Editions Maeght, Paris

6 *Guitare et Compotier*
1908, oil on canvas
21½ × 15 in (55 × 38 cm)
Kunstmuseum, Bern

never put himself first. He spoke through symbols and maxims. In his writings he is never autobiographical. His private life was deliberately the biography of his work. In his work he effaced himself, yet only within it could he recognise himself. To follow the course of his life means to follow the course of his painting. It means to reconstruct the development of his extraordinary craft.

His apprenticeship began with the transfer of his family from Argenteuil to Le Havre in 1890; Braque was then eight years old. He worked in his father's decorating shop, during which time he followed evening courses at the Ecole des Beaux-Arts.

One of his few biographical reminiscences was his interest as a child in the life of the port, which was to leave an important imprint on his work, as it had already on that of Monet, Dufy and Othon Freisz, who had also visited Le Havre. But it was above all his work in his father's shop and in that of another *peintre-décorateur,* named Roncy, that was the determining factor for Braque. He always attributed great importance to the technical perfection of his work, taking up in this way the old idea of the artist as a specialist, as both theoretician and technician. This idea goes back to the anti-historical rationalism of Canova, but had been lost in the rigorous empiricism of the Impressionists with their positivist, scientific outlook. It was only rediscovered and once more acquired an independent meaning with Cézanne. (Cézanne wrote 'I had decided to work in silence until the day when I would be capable of theoretically justifying my work'.)

It should be made clear that Braque did not take this perfection as a matter of routine but as a working method, as a means to awareness, as a 'rational' fact; this was to be the basis of the conception of the artist in the modern world. For it constituted the only alternative to the anonymity of standardisation under industrial capitalism; an alternative in which a new and unique possibility for the existence of art and its function in society becomes synthesised.

At the museum in Le Havre young Braque studied Boudin, Corot (who remained, as we shall see, one of his references), and Toulouse-Lautrec. At the same time he frequented the theatre and learned to play the flute (taught by Gaston Dufy, the brother of Raoul). By the end of 1900 (at eighteen) he was in Paris where he pursued his technical studies at an artisan level. He was a pupil of Laberthe and attended the municipal art course at Batignolles; here he perfected himself as a *peintre-décorateur,* was trained to reproduce false marbles, precious woods and wallpapers, and to prepare colours, backgrounds and other painting materials.

This technical ability and pictorial approach, transformed on to a level of intellectual and cultural significance, was later to be put to use in the realisation of one of Braque's most fundamental pictorial innovations; the Cubist collages of 1911.

Figs. 1, 2 · To this period belongs his Impressionist experience. However, it was in relation to the Fauves that Braque began to reveal, through his highly personal adhesion to the movement, the originality of his approach to painting.

From 1905 to 1906 he was a neighbour of Othon Friesz, first at Antwerp and then at L'Estaque on the Mediterranean coast (in the midst of Cézanne's landscape, though Braque had not yet seen Cézanne as his true master). Here Fig. 3 he worked out the meaning of the anti-Impressionist reaction of the Fauves, based on colour, which he in fact was already using as a structural feature in his paintings, as the plastic element in pictorial construction.

For examples of his work from this period we may cite *Anvers: Les* Pls. 1, 2 *Bateaux Pavoisés* (1905–6, Kunstmuseum, Basle) and *Le Port de L'Estaque* (1906–7, private collection, Zurich).

The arrangement of the colours, painted in sharp, clear strokes, is based on a scheme which provides the compositional and structural pattern of these two paintings (of which there are several variations). In the second, this pattern takes a more intense form, expressed in a subtle fragmentation of light. The disposition of the mass of colours, red, yellow, green, blue and deep violet, is clear and clean. This arrangement of separate brushstrokes produces a continuous subtle shimmering effect and a kind of chromatic incandescence. (At the end of 1904 after having discovered the Impressionists–Renoir, Monet, Sisley, Pissaro–Braque discovered above all, Van Gogh and the 'tachism' of Seurat.)

The composition is already developed through planes: 'Visual space,' he wrote, 'separates objects one from the other.' This was Braque's continual preoccupation which led him to upset the perspective based on the horizontal plane of the picture, tilting it forward. Van Gogh had already done the same by developing the characteristic feature of Dutch painting, the uplifting of the horizontal line. This was eventually to lead to the complete reduction of perspective distance in the Cubist vision.

But Fauvism and the expression of his personal being, which it involved, could not satisfy the need for balance and discipline which Braque had inherited from the French tradition. The close relationship between Braque and Chardin, typically emphasised by the French critics, is not accidental; it refers to distinctive common features. However, if we consider the question in cultural rather than 'ethnic' terms the names one could indicate as 'elective affinities' would point to the international cultural projection of Braque's work in the future rather than its antecedents in the past. We could, for example, cite the work of Ben Nicholson, or the Italian painter Morandi. It is more a question of legitimate descendants than ancestors.

7 *La Roche Guyon: le Château*
1909, oil on canvas
$32 \times 23\frac{1}{2}$ in (81×60 cm)
Rolf de Maré collection, Stockholm

Fauvism exalted the personality of the artist almost in the form of a paroxism, releasing the pictorial instinct as a primordial force. It represented ultimately the negation of all rules. It ran the risk of becoming academicism in reverse, exulting in gratuitousness and total disorder.

It was his discovery of the master of Aix (at the 1907 Paris retrospective of Cézanne, organised by Bernheim-Jeune) which revealed to Braque the true path he was to follow.

Cézanne had altered the very terms of the pictorial problem. He defined the picture in conceptual terms, which he deduced aesthetically and technically from the painting alone. For him, painting was volumetric representation of reality by means of colour, discovered through his own experience and knowledge as a man and as an artist. His need to justify his work theoretically shows that, for him, this theoretical approach was never *a priori,* but was always reached through discovered awareness and experience of reality. The fact that this reality or vision of the world is synthesised in the painting and identified with it, only confirms the responsibility of the artist for his own image of the world.

For Cézanne the picture was constructed on parallel planes, graduated from foreground to background to indicate depth.

Maurice Gieure writes: 'It is likely that Braque's visual space which

Visual space

8 *Petite Guitare Cubiste*
1909, etching, 1954 print
$5\frac{1}{2} \times 8$ in (14×20 cm)
Editions Maeght, Paris

"separates objects one from another" derives directly from here.'[5] Braque himself was to write: 'I was very much struck by Cézanne's paintings, which I had seen at Vollard's; I felt that there was something significant hidden in his pictures.'[6]

In Braque's work, Cézanne's rhythmical space was to lose its illusive depth and to approach more and more the surface of the canvas, until it became merged with it. Space thus became compact and enclosed, a tangible link between objects, or what Braque called 'tactile space', the space which 'separates itself from objects'.

The painting as object

The compromise between the man and his work thereby became absolute; the anonymity of the author is sealed by the autonomy of the picture as a completely independent 'object', quite separate from himself. This also explains the fusion of styles which characterises the first Cubist phase of Braque and Picasso. The discovery of Cézanne served in fact as a catalyst in the meeting between Braque and Picasso organised by Kahnweiler and Apollinaire. Picasso had at that point just finished *Les Demoiselles d'Avignon* (October, 1907). This painting combined his chief interests at the time— primitive art, Catalan Romanesque, African sculpture and the work of Cézanne. *Les Demoiselles* provoked in Braque a fundamental sense of shock (as he later put it; 'an effect of revulsion').

It undoubtedly represents the immediate source for his *Grand Nu* (1907, collection Madame Cuttoli, Paris). In this painting we can discern a greater fluidity in the relationship between volumes, a more direct fusion, a softer dissolving of colours into each other, features which already denote the difference between Braque's approach and Picasso's. From this work we can date the collaboration between the two artists in relation to Cubism,

5 M. Gieure, *Georges Braque,* Paris, 1956.
6 G. Braque, *La peinture et nous: propos de l'artiste,* edited by Dora Vallier, Basle, 1962.

which itself coincided with their relationship and represents one of the most important and decisive events of the cultural life of our century.

In the *Grand Nu* the overturning of planes, the multiple viewpoints and the volumetric definition of space prefigure the 1908 canvases painted at L'Estaque and those of 1909 at La Roche Guyon. Besides representing a complete revision of Cézanne's discoveries, these mark a direct step towards Cubism; they run parallel to Picasso's work at the same time at *La Rue des Bois* on the Oise and at Horta de Ebro in Spain, affording striking similarities and coincidences. At the end of the summer of 1908 Braque was once more at L'Estaque, this time in search of Cézanne's landscapes.

The splendid series of landscapes painted at L'Estaque show the definition of certain premises already recognisable in the paintings of the Fauve period; there is no longer a single trace of linear perspective, nor of spatial depth. (Of this series reproduced here are one from the Museum of Modern Art, Paris, and one from the Kunstmuseum, Basle; others are to be found in Bern, Copenhagen and New York.) The line of the horizon is raised to the disappearing point, the sky is repressed, vivid colour has given way to an amalgam of purplish greys, straw-like ochres and browns in a sort of tonal monochrome of compact zones divided by boundaries of mute greens. 'The succession of clear and dark surfaces broken into sharp angles, delineating for each volume its point of focus without any central convergence, accentuate the spatial illusion.'[7]

The refusal of these works by the *Salon d'Automne* was a sign of official hostility in reaction to these new developments in his work. (Braque had always shown at the *Salon des Indépendants* and had always been successful. The works of the Fauve period had all been sold.) Matisse, a member of the commission for the selection of works, said '*Trop de cubes!*'

On the other hand, a group of intellectuals and poets was beginning to

Fig. 4

9 *Nature Morte Cubiste*
1912, etching, 1953 print
13 × 18 in (33 × 45·5 cm)
Editions Maeght, Paris

Pl. 3
Pl. 4

7 J. Leymaire, *Braque,* Geneva, 1961.

gather around the two protagonists of the new artistic movement. Gertrude Stein and her brother Leo Stein, Guillaume Apollinaire, Max Jacob, Cendrars, Reverdie (particularly friendly with Braque) and finally Valéry. After the Salon refusal, the young collector Kahnweiler responded by organising the first Braque show at his gallery, introduced by Guillaume Apollinaire; this was to be the first Cubist exhibition. The review 'Gil Blas' of the 14th November, 1908, carried the declaration of Louis Vauxcelles, the critic to whose incomprehension we owe two useful definitions: that of 'Fauves' referring to the *Salon d'Automne* of 1905, where works had been shown by Matisse, Marquet, Manguin, Puy, Valtat, Vlaminck, Derain, Vondongen, Freisz; and that of 'Cubism'. Vauxcelles wrote in *Gil Blas*: 'M. Braque is a very audacious man. He despises form and reduces everything, settings, houses and figures, to geometrical schemes, to *cubes*.' And later added: 'cubist oddities.'

Fig. 7   In 1909 Braque painted a series of eight pictures at La Roche-Guyon, a village on the banks of the river Seine, dominated from above by the castle of La Rochefoucauld. Here too the sky has vanished. The white image of a crystal palace is once again transposed in terms of spatial allusion in the different variations it makes.

The geometrical forms that Braque had already begun in his still-lifes in 1908, which constituted the basic theme of Cubism, were realised more and more. The first of the still-lifes was *La Nature Morte aux Instruments de Musique* (Musée National d'Art Moderne, Paris) of 1908, a harmony of curved and angular masses with corresponding sombre chromatic chords of ochre and green, cold and hot tones (already foreshadowing the multiple vision of objects through the opening and destruction of planes). Repro-

Pl. 5   duced here is the splendid *Violon et Cruche*, 1910 (Kunstmuseum, Basle), which plays on the subtle, vibrating tension and interaction between multi-faceted planes, like solid crystals, all of the same inorganic nature.

The pitcher, violin and table define themselves in a solid and transparent atmosphere; the whole is as compact as a crystalline geological formation, clouded by a delicate monochrome in tones of brown; the shadows efface the definition of planes with protruding volumes at the same time as they create them. The entire composition is projected forward towards the plane of the canvas; the images re-echo each other within their multi-faceted surfaces, in a suggestive dynamic repeated with successive rhythmic super-impositions, in distorted sequence, almost reflected in sound waves trans-mitted by the instrument in the foreground. ('The container gives form to emptiness, music to silence.') This seems to be a prelude to the dynamism (also in a Cubist key) of the *Nude Descending a Staircase* of Marcel Duchamp, 1911 (Museum of Art, Philadelphia).

In these still-lifes, which form the whole of the first period of Cubism (that is, Analytical Cubism), from 1908 to 1911, reference to naturalistic appearance is gradually abandoned. The objects are welded to each other, solidifying the surrounding atmosphere in a manner which seems pro-gressively suffocating to the space and background.

The same process is found in the landscapes. For example in *L'Usine du*

Pl. 6   *Rio Tinto à L'Estaque* (Musée National d'Art Moderne, Paris) we can still trade the influence of Cézanne in the attitude towards volume; however this work already shows the eradication of volumetric articulation of relationships. The composition is developed through superimposed, juxta-posed and intersected planes; it is built up in zones which are not always distinguished geometrically. The surfaces are not clearly defined in terms of colour, tone, or shading and each slides into the next without either thematic or hierarchical distinction. All the volumes, compact and opaque, and all the empty spaces, perforated, compressible and fluid, become merged. The earth and sky, houses and air, objects and their surrounding space have the same consistency, the same density.

Pl. 7   In *Composition au Violon*, 1911 (Musée National d'Art Moderne, Paris), the obliteration of the scansion of volumes is even more evident. This is seen in

10 *Aria de Bach*
1912–13, charcoal drawing and
collage on paper
24½ × 18 in (62 × 46 cm)
M. Cuttoli collection, Paris

the treatment of the surface of the painting. Braque uses small white alternating brush-strokes (more indefinite towards the greater density at the centre of the image); the oblique running away of lines, which unravel into disappearing rays, create tension towards the edges around the central, more representational block, as if echoing the successive presence of the objects in different zones of the space. The white strokes dissolve the instruments and the human image, which itself becomes an object among others, a still-life, a mere pretext for a composition.

During these years, therefore, Braque was not searching for volumetric space, the illusory plasticity of figuration; rather, he was deepening the possibilities offered by the pictorial surface. This still remained the problem of pure painting.

In this period he managed to surpass the traditional limits of the picture frame, defined by straight lines; he restored the oval edge which 'eliminates *a priori* all analogous correlations between the physical limits of the painting and the traditional schema of "cubic" space based on perspective'.[8]

At this point Braque began to insert letters of the alphabet as well as numbers, used as symbols of a new vocabulary. Of course, the inserted letters lose their traditional symbolism, taking on a new semantic meaning. They become conventional signs of communication differing from spoken

8 G. C. Argan, *Braque,* New York, Amsterdam, Milan, 1957.

11 *Nature Morte aux Racines*
1927, signed at bottom right
oil on canvas
$8 \times 11\frac{1}{2}$ in (21 × 29 cm)
Philips collection, Washington

and written language. They represent an analogous correlation with reality, a new means of engaging with the real world through the filter of the artist's experience. For Braque they were real and 'undeformable' forms, existing only in the painting, outside real space, objects without dimension – the exact transcription of reality into the only dimension, that of the picture.

'Things do not exist in themselves at all; they exist only through our interpretation.'

Pl. 8   In *Le Portugais,* 1911 (Kunstmuseum, Basle), outlined planes are dominant. The rhythm develops through the joining and superimposition of flat elements, a harmony of folded pages supported by subtle forms and colours. ('Form and colour do not merge. They are simultaneous,' said Braque.) The almost uniform ochre-grey tone is assaulted here and there by cutting shafts of deeper and denser brown.

Pl. 9   Another admirable example of this achievement of equilibrium, of limpid harmony, and expressive clarity is *Le Guéridon,* 1911–12 (Musée National d'Art Moderne, Paris). This piece is filled with an incredible sweetness; the objects now cast a luminous shadow, almost a quintessence, the poetic result of their existence in the human world. This is possibly one of Braque's most absolute works. The theme of the small round table was to be taken up more often later in the form of a revived naturalism. But even so, it still represents a mere object-pretext, an absolute protagonist; like the famous fruit bowl in Cubist still-lifes it becomes a 'Christ image of the twentieth century', as defined by Derain.

Tactile space   Until this time Braque had been proving in his work the significance of his definition of visual space, which 'separates objects from one another',

12 *Nature Morte; Le Jour*
1929, signed at bottom right
oil on canvas
$44\frac{1}{2} \times 56\frac{1}{2}$ in (113 × 144 cm)
Chester Dale collection,
National Gallery, Washington

transforming space into a form of the same consistency as the objects themselves. From this stage onwards he was concerned to prove his second assertion: 'that tactile space separates the object from itself'. Berenson alludes to these 'tactile values' when he writes: 'they exist in representation of solid objects, when they are communicated in such a manner as to solicit the imagination to feel their volume, to weigh them in one's hands, to make one aware of their potential resistance, to measure the space which separates them, encouraging one, still in the imagination, to join close contact with them, to catch them, to pull them or to move around them.'[9]

Braque was the first artist of the contemporary world to mix into his colour sand, ashes, rope, metal filings, even tobacco, to vary the material and give the colour more body. By means of linguistic transposition he once again became the creator of an object.

It is in this sense that we can appreciate the introduction of *papier collé* into the painting. (Picasso had already initiated the use of collage.) This insertion of real material into the painting asserted the absolute autonomy of the artist's own means of expression, in painting and in art generally.

'In the painting the contrast of materials has the same value as the contrast of colours. I use a variety of materials, and the colours take on a much more intense significance and more extended variety. With a transparent lacquer and opaque ochre one can achieve, for example, a harmonious effect; in other words opposites can be juxtaposed like colours.'

'In the end, what is colour? Saying red or green one says nothing. If one is dealing with blood red it is one thing or brick red, another, and so on *ad infinitum*. What a difference!'

9 J. Richardson, *Georges Braque,* London, 1961.

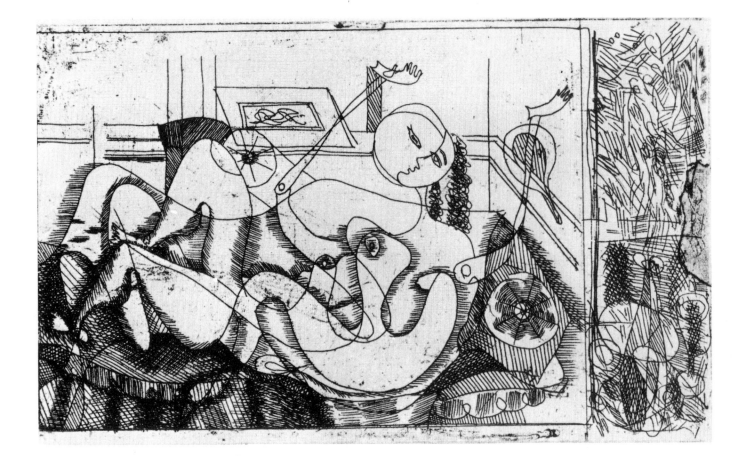

13 *Nu Allongé*
1934, etching for 'G. Braque'
by Carl Einstein
7 × 12 in (18 × 30 cm)

14 *Le Duo*
1937, signed at bottom left
oil on canvas
39 × 52 in (100 × 130 cm)
Musée National d'Art Moderne,
Paris

15 *Vanitas*
1939, signed at bottom left
oil and sand on canvas
15 × 13¾ in (38 × 35 cm)
Musée National d'Art Moderne
Paris

Pl. 10

Pl. 11

Fig. 10
Pls. 12, 13

At this point Braque began transferring to his work the results of his youthful training, the virtuosities of the *peintre-décorateur*. He began juxtaposing or replacing the *papier collé,* pieces of paper representing false marble or false wood, with pieces of pictorial *bravura,* imitations of *papier collé,* wood, marble and so on, thus creating a *trompe l'œil* effect. This operation was, of course, quite distinct from the routine skills he had originally learned; the change of context and purpose of the whole gave it an entirely fresh significance. It was also, finally, a means of raising a craft skill to the level of intellectual professionalism.

The second phase of Cubism, or 'Synthetic Cubism', began with the use of collage and *papier collé.*

In this period the process of decomposition of the object into planes was transformed by the inverse process. The surfaces are all reduced down to one flat plane, of a uniform colour, without any trace of shadow or gradation. They appear as a stylised moulding of the object, which moreover, becomes recognisable through the delineation of outlines. The colour once more becomes vivid, and space is reasserted as a factor external to the object, creating 'a field of relationships and tensions'.[10] The *papier collé* is reduced to pictorial material, with colour spread across it as in *Le Quotidien, Violon et Pipe,* 1912 (Musée National d'Art Moderne, Paris). Signs and undulating lines unite the *papier collé* with the rest of the composition, merging it within the whole. This transforms the *papier collé* into pictorial material, as in *Composition à l'As de Trèfle* (1912–13, Musée National d'Art Moderne, Paris). In this instance the object becomes an insignia, hewn out of a field of forces, evoking its presence with allusive directness (playing cards, the wood of the table, the white plate). Instead of the formation of bright and solid crystals, the fragmented moulds meet on flat planes (the plate or playing card of inserted false wood do not appear any less fragmented). Musical allusions are frequent ('I am always drawn to paint objects which are animated by touch alone'): *Aria de Bach* 1912–13 (Roche collection, Paris); *La Table du Musicien,* 1913 (Kunstmuseum, Basle); *La Clarinette,* 1913 (private collection, New York); *Femme à la Guitare,* 1913 (Musée National

10 U. Apollonio, *Braque,* Milan, 1967.

d'Art Moderne, Paris). The last of these takes up once more a theme already broached by Picasso in 1911.

Pl. 14   In *Verre et Violon*, 1913–14 (Kunstmuseum, Basle), the plane is interwoven with superimpositions, intersections, and variations on flat symbols of objects. The colour recovers here certain modulations of the 'Synthetic' period, based on subtle monotone relationships between white-brown and white-grey.

Pl. 15   *Verre, Bouteille et Pipe sur une Table,* 1914 (Mattioli collection, Milan), marks, according to a formula which Braque often adopts, a return and redevelopment of previous themes. The style of 'Analytical' Cubism (of 'scientific' Cubism as Apollinaire) is expressed in the amalgam of a flecked ground, made up of flat signs on a flat surface.

In this composition a sort of *guéridon* table once more appears, thrust forward, revealing its round linear surface (half *papier collé,* half painted). The objects are composed of multiple planes disappearing ultimately into the flat background.

The years of obsession

In 1914 Braque's association with Picasso came to an end; this had been so close that their themes and solutions had often been identical, so much so that only extremely attentive observation can at times distinguish their work. Braque, good Frenchman that he was, went to war, fought gloriously, was wounded in the head and had to have his skull trepanned.

At least three years passed before he was able to resume work. On his return Paris had greatly changed. Picasso, far away, was following his own path. Only Juan Gris, of so many followers, had remained faithful to Cubism. In the years following the war the two artists were quite close.

Pl. 16   In *La Musicienne,* 1917–18 (Kunstmuseum, Basle), the rigour of synthetic Cubism is expressed by compact rigidity, by an altogether new firmness. The different planes are resolved into zones of firm colour in a unitary vertical rhythm fixed on a stable basis. Even the shape of the canvas is unusual, long and narrow; from now on this was to be Braque's favourite dimension, the long rectangle divided horizontally or vertically.

The resulting image is sybilline and disturbing, almost a sacred monster, divinely remote from the human world. The variation of treatment is weighed up with the accuracy and the clarity of an absolute vision. ('A picture is finished when it has cancelled the idea.') In several passages one can see flat areas of colour (chalk white, shining dark red, brown, blue and black), *papier collé* in the area of the floor, with insertions of painted *trompe l'œil* and false wood juxtaposed with speckled areas, which serve a decorative function against the varied background.

In *La Musicienne* the composition is objectified by the sense of calm attained, by the sense of Olympic completeness. This image is perhaps more naturalistic; but, precisely because it is placed beyond the reach of emotion it has, more than any other in Braque's work, its own alert force, its mental presence and its own inexorability, almost terrifying.

The more intense range of colours of this period is also emphasised by the backgrounds, dark or even black; these have a capacity to evoke depth without necessarily implying distance. The still-lifes, composed of flat forms, appear to rise out of the surface as from a void.

The artist seems to have rediscovered the significance of the fragment, by a lucid selection of shreds of reality which can evoke human presence; for

Pl. 17   example in *Clarinette, Guitare et Compotier,* 1918 (Kunstmuseum, Basle), each fragmentary object plays an evocative role; flat zones of colour, somewhat mute, are alternated with zones of material, false cloths, false woods, in a kind of sensitive patchwork, a poetic transposition of traditional everyday domestic life. The result evokes the feeling of objects modelled by the human hand, by the long use which has gradually transformed them; a kind of household panorama, continually within reach of the eye and the hand ('It is not sufficient that what is painted should be seen; it is necessary to make it tangible').

In *Café Bar,* 1919 (Kunstmuseum, Basle), the Cubist aesthetic is still recognisable, but this work already clearly represents a departure. The space is developed through planes which cross, superimpose, intersect. The vertical rhythm, which articulate the small table (still a *guéridon*) and the objects upon it, is broken up by horizontal tensions (sketched-in white tassles, cords and the suggestion of an accordion). The tones are grey and black with brown reflections, very dark.

'As in Picasso the tonality of the painting is the plastic sum of the objects. The objects are pretexts or motifs for the totality of their representation which could be described in the following formula: the object from the

Pl. 18

16 *Hélios*
1946, lithograph
$20 \times 16\frac{1}{2}$ in ($50 \cdot 5 \times 42$ cm)

Figs. 17, 19, 20

Figs. 16, 22

Pl. 20

front + the object from the side + the object in section + the object from above + the object from below, etc., to which one could add, flat rhythm of the object — curved rhythm of the object. The difference with Picasso lies in the fact that there is no plastic emphasis on recognisable forms and relationships of proximity are not limited to the objects.

'The objects are enveloped in a space, which is itself objectified, rhythmic and saturated; the large grey-black quadrilateral, the colour tones of the guitar, of the fruit bowl, of the fruit, of the small table, of the newspaper; the greys and blacks of the background in turn depend on fragments of musical notation and the pipe. Everything that Braque has painted up to the present (1956) is already to be found here, whether present or in potential form.'[11]

Braque's tactile perfection is also based on extremely careful preparation of the canvas. ('The priming of the canvas is the basis of everything, as are the foundations of a house.')

The canvases from 1920 onwards are prepared with a thick, opaque layer, rough and black; Braque has compared this preparation to coffee grounds or used tea leaves, since in it he can, as if telling his future, 'predict things that others cannot see'.

Even in his graphic work, he sometimes uses deep backgrounds; through a progressive darkening he succeeds in obtaining a firmer relief of the object. As an example of this we may note passages in three successive stages of a beautiful lithography of a later date (1946) *La Théière et les Pommes* (reproduced here in black and white). Sometimes, still by graphic means, he worked on extremely dense backgrounds, almost like bas-reliefs, by etching into them, as in a series of illustrations for Hesiod's *Theogony* (1950) composed of arabesques of fluid continuous lines.

By 1920 Braque was working on these specially primed and prepared backgrounds achieving extraordinary effects with transparent materials, diaphanous or opaque. This period can be compared to the 'classical' period of Picasso, that of Canaphores, in which monumental figures, taken from the Greek repertory, carriers of fruit basket trailing with flowers, are treated as large still-lifes. They glow with evanescent colour, serving both as a decorative motif and a solar symbol of warm, full sensuality. We reproduce from this period a large caryatid (1922, Musée National d'Art Moderne, Paris), her torso sustained by severe and ample forms, resembling an ancient goddess of fertility. The Canaphores period of Picasso continued until 1927, running parallel to Braque's series of gueridons, in its successive variations and styles. These continued to follow the tendency of monu-

11 M. Gieure *op. cit.*

26

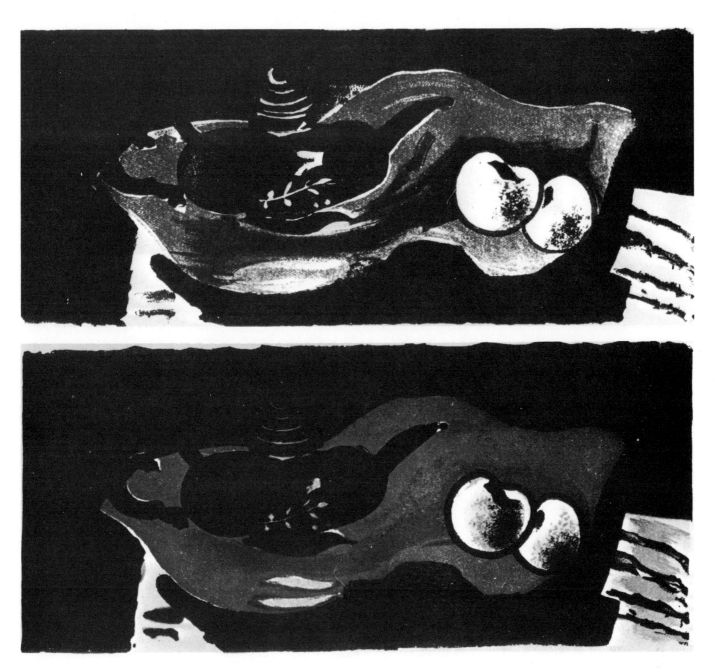

mental exaltation of the object ('Christ images of the twentieth century'), which reappeared in later periods, from 1939 (see the work of 1939–52 in the Galerie National d'Art Moderne in Paris) as if to test a new linguistic approach, based on the 'sign', to demonstrate the integrity of certain themes and motifs. This integrity had to be tested and re-established in terms of changes in his own practice.

On this question of Braque's concern for the integrity of his paintings, though seen here against an external reality, Reverdy recounts: 'In 1917 I met him in the South, near Avignon, and one day as we went across the fields from Sorgues to the cottage where I lived, Braque carried one of his paintings on a stick slung over his shoulder. We made a stop. Braque laid the painting on the ground between some pebbles and grass. I was astonished by what he said: "It is extraordinary how this 'holds true' against real colour and against the stones." Later he told me that it was important above all to find out whether his work would "hold out" even in a famine. Today I can reply: yes, they hold out against so many things, because they are not afraid of anything.'[12]

In the *Guéridons* series, until 1927–8 as Leymarie has observed, geometrical rigidity disappeared. Indented planes and flexible curves uplift the exuberant mass of objects creating an association between them and the rhythm of the background. The rich pictorial substance which unifies

19 *La Théière et les Pommes*
1946, lithograph in seven colours
$11\frac{1}{2} \times 25\frac{1}{2}$ in (29 × 65 cm)
second proof

20 *Théière et les Pommes*
1946, lithograph in seven colours
$11\frac{1}{2} \times 25\frac{1}{2}$ in (29 × 65 cm)
third proof

12 J. Leymaire *op. cit.*

form, colour and material, reaches that fullness which by now is characteristic of Braque (as if all his future work was already present within these paintings); Paulhan defines this singular quality as: 'Fluid (without needing water); radiant (without the slightest source of light); dramatic (without pretence).' Picasso placed his extraordinary *Guéridons* before windows open to the sky of Dinard or St. Raphael; Braque, decidedly claustrophobic like Chardin, did not place a single open window in his painting until 1938 (Juan Gris had done so in 1915, and Picasso in 1919). Braque did not, until he had conquered, progressively and tangibly, the corresponding space within the room. His light emanates from the movement of hot and cold, light and dark tones; it represents a deaf phosphorescence, tied to the material nature of the object rather than to external illumination.[13] Many still-lifes date from this period, developed horizontally and in low and

Pl. 22   large forms such as the *Nature Morte aux Poires* (Musée National d'Art Moderne, Paris).

Pl. 21   But also from this period is *Souvenir de Corot*, 1922–3 (Musée National d'Art Moderne, Paris). Since his early youth Braque had admired Corot, and the exhibition of twenty-four Corot portraits at the Salon d'Automne of 1909 had brought his name into the limelight. This *Souvenir* is not a copy, but rather a variation on one of his favourite themes. One can compare it

Fig. 18   with Corot's *Portrait of Christine Nilsson*, 1874 (Museu de Arte, São Paulo), reproduced here in black and white. Here Braque reaffirms his predilection for painting interiors; these contain pictures hung on the walls (the painting-

Pl. 35   within-the-painting was to reappear as one of the themes of the *Ateliers* series). But this painting is also an example of Braque's interpretation of the human figure, not so much naturalistic as, rather, a tonal modulation of pictorial space in an intimate sense, a homage to the best French tradition.

This is also the period of the splendid *Cheminées* series, which continued until 1927. (Among the best known are: that of 1922, Weil collection, St Louis; that of 1923, Kunsthaus, Zurich; that of 1925, Marx collection, Chicago; and that of 1925, Norton Gallery, West Palm Beach.) In the *Cheminées* a return to the use of perspective is evident at times. However, the treatment of materials in the fireplace–in particular, marble, which is often reproduced realistically–and other objects superimposed, tends to create again the feeling of a suspended plane. This is trapped in a dense atmosphere in which objects expand but remain arrested, as if drowned. We are still a long way from the spatial dimension of the *Ateliers* period when space becomes reaffirmed as a spiritual dimension. Objects then become freed from their restriction within an atmosphere of the same consistency as themselves; they tear themselves free, float and expand in mid-air, in 'liquid' air, as if in an aquarium.

The Sorgues period

Pl. 24   In the meantime, Braque continued to produce variations and resumptions in his still-lifes, including collections of flowers ás in *Anémones dans un Vase*, 1927 (Roger Varenne collection, Geneva). These are works which can be called naturalistic. With their toned-down ochres and softness of treatment they evoke a kind of gentle sensuality which Braque rarely reserves for the human figure. In the *Baigneuses* of this period and in *Femme Couchée*, 1930–52 (Musée National d'Art Moderne, Paris), calligraphic stylisation and sumptuous elegance render all the more remote and secret the cold sensuality which underlies them. It becomes more evident in his lovely linear drawings in which the line becomes a pure euphoric arabesque. We can also find the same gentle and ironic passion in certain drawings by Klee. Aside from his graphic work, one can find this quality in a few of the purer still-lifes (it should however not be overlooked that their treatment is almost graphic). Two are reproduced here; *Grande Nature Morte Brune*, 1931 (Musée National

Pls. 25, 26   d'Art Moderne, Paris) and *Nature Morte à la Pipe*, 1932–4 (Kunstmuseum, Basle).

The change of style in this period coincided with a change in the environ-

13 J. Leymaire *op. cit.*

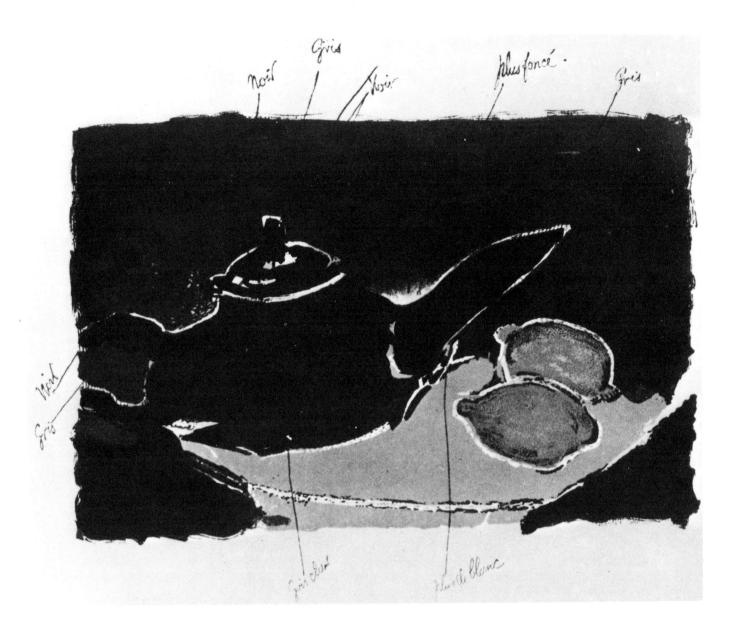

21 *Théière et Citrons*
1949, lithograph in five colours
on transparent lithographic paper
$14 \times 17\frac{1}{4}$ in (36×44 cm)
first proof

ment of his life. This is natural, since for Braque his life coincides with and completely feeds itself into his work.

Braque was now tired of the light of southern France, of the violent consistency of objects, of their matter—and hence pictorial material—which that light so crudely reveals. He left Sorgues where, apart from the three war years, he had spent all his summers since he went there the day after his marriage in 1912, and moved to Varengeville near Dieppe. The colder, more crystalline light and the fresher, more precise vision of objects was reflected in the basic transparency of his new pictorial vision.

These still-lifes, reduced to linear signs, were developed in a similar manner to the graphic work of this period. This was done with ample drawing, in harmonious curves in which the objects, by now only evoked, are transformed into coloured flat surfaces. (In fact, they follow the earlier thickly incised paintings, which evoked Greek vase painting, and the illustrations for the *Theogony*.) The intersection of planes does not hide the contours of the objects, which are marked with subtle white lines. They represent, as Argan writes, 'a profound meditation on the value of the sign, on the absolute equivalence which can be established in terms of pure painting, between large areas of colour, and a slight black mark on white or white on black. In fact, in terms of pure painting, there is no reason to believe that a large zone of colour has more spatial significance than a line'.[14] This seems to arise from a reconsideration of the linear style of Matisse.

As we have seen, the new *Guéridons* develop according to a linear rhythm in the joy of a newly discovered 'sign'. (Reproduced here is that of 1939–52,   Pl. 27

14 G. C. Argan *op. cit.*

29

22 Illustration for
Hesiod's *Theogony*
1946, etching
$11\frac{1}{2} \times 9\frac{1}{2}$ in ($29 \cdot 5 \times 24$ cm)

23 Ceiling of the Etruscan Hall,
the Louvre, number 1
1953, oil on canvas
83×107 in (211×272 cm)

Musée National d'Art Moderne, Paris.) This appears to be symbolised in
the refined elegance of the subtle interweaving of the three curved table legs.

The Varengeville period

From 1933 to 1940–1 Braque's activity, already rich with the achievements
of much work and much meditation (his 'obsession') still largely consisted of
still-lifes: *La Nappe Rose,* 1933 (New York, W. P. Chrysler collection);
La Nappe Jaune, 1935 (Chicago, Samuel A. Marx collection); *La Nappe
Mauve,* 1936 (New York, Mrs Albert D. Lasker collection). These paintings
develop the theme of interiors, resolving it with a spatial form which
recreates a king of perspective in new form.

In 1937, the human figure is reinserted into his interiors, *Femme à la
Mandoline,* 1937 (Museum of Modern Art, New York); *Le Peintre et son
Modèle,* 1939 (New York, Walter P. Chrysler Jr collection, etc.). These
involve a particular interpretation of the figure; thread-like manikins,
double silhouettes, half-light, half-dark, arranged into an admonishing
presence, like presentiments of a drama which will take humanity by sur-
prise. They are abstract personages, but are not too far or detached from
life; they are no longer the silent idols of the distant *Musicienne* of 1917.
Here the tragedy, the drama unfurling over Europe, is lucidly presented,
but with great suffering.

In May, 1940, at the moment of the German invasion, Braque was at
Varengeville. He took refuge for a few months in Limousin, then in the
Pyrenees, but in the autumn moved back to Paris, which he did not leave
again, even during the occupation.

The 'interiors'

Still attached to every-day objects, the only possible salvation for a beseiged
humanity, he sought refuge once more in his favourite theme, his still-lifes.
In these he tried to reconquer a sense of plasticity which would make them
less abstract, more direct and within reach, as in *Le Pain,* 1940–1 (Musée
National d'Art Moderne, Paris), or in *L'Entonnoir,* 1941 (George Waeghter
Memorial Foundation, Geneva). In these he seemed to be searching, with
all his might, for a more simple, more direct treatment of objects, almost
reconstructed in a new open plasticity. *La Patience* of 1942 (S. Jaffé collection,
Beverly Hills), is an enigmatic figure with a double profile, both nocturnal
and solar, mysterious and omniscient.

But the space in these new interiors, where windows have already been
opened on to disquieting skies, *La Table de Toilette,* 1942 (Musée National
d'Art Moderne, Paris), conquers a new dimension. The atmosphere becomes
brighter, and is no longer compact and dense. For example, see *Le Salon,*

Pls. 28, 29

Pl. 30

Pl. 31

24 *Le Nid, ou Oiseau*
1955, etching
$8\frac{3}{4} \times 14\frac{1}{2}$ in $(22 \cdot 5 \times 37$ cm)
Editions Maeght, Paris

Pl. 32

Pl. 33

25 *Vol de Nuit*
1957, lithograph
16×27 in $(41 \times 69$ cm)
Editions Maeght, Paris

26 *L'Qiseau traversant le Nuage*
1957, lithograph
16×27 in $(41 \times 69$ cm)
Editions Maeght, Paris

1944 (Musée National d'Art Moderne, Paris). Here the window is the central focus of the composition, external light is transformed into internal light; to the right is a new sumptuous *guéridon* covered by a very dark rug, the undulating folds of which are indicated by white parallel lines. At the centre, small blue flowers in a vase create a very gentle presence. He has completely recaptured the every-day dimension; it is 1944; possibly peace enabled him to enter the world again.

The atmosphere becomes more rarefied and is now allowed to filter through objects. The objects themselves in the works of this period often become transparent and allusive, more from an external viewpoint than in relation to themselves. In *Le Billard,* 1945 (Musée National d'Art Moderne, Paris), the table becomes an allusion to the artist's easel, an ambivalent transparent mould folded in half.

Here however the atmosphere is becoming empty; the tense and interwoven lines of perspective are absurdly fractured, and turn the recreated perspective upside down, breaking the billiard-table in two, which seems to resound with the dry crackling of the sudden rupture. The wall at the back, empty and taut like the table itself, and placed in the same position, broken and folded at an angle into a forced pleat, seems like an even larger and more desolate table. Realistic annotations—the grates of the window, the mouldings of the fixtures and cornices, the rings from which, on a long post to the extreme left, hangs a braided cord—all are inexorable testimonies of a bewitched reality. In 1948 Braque painted *La Chaise de Jardin* (Musée National d'Art Moderne, Paris), which is a metal chair seen as a profile in the very foreground of the painting, like an allusive ideogram (rather like Van Gogh's chair). It is an amazing piece of bravura. The drawing ornamented with arabesques, stands out against the material surface, a golden ochre, traversed by shimmering light. This is a *squelette exquise* of an unreal humanity, and like its product, is both dazed and secure, gentle and aggressive. It is not a symbol; it is humanity itself. At the same time, with the objects upon it (a basket of fruit) it is the ultimate still-life. Perhaps it is only in such an allusive transposition of significance that one can speak, in relation

to Braque, of surrealism. But one is dealing with a very particular type of surrealism, not heavy or visionary but in a certain sense animistic. For Braque the object is existentially the same as man.

This is possibly what Braque wished to say when he stated that he did not express himself through symbols but rather through 'metamorphosis'. 'The only valid thing in art is that which one cannot explain,' he said. He later wrote: 'In my own work there are mysteries and secrets which even I do not understand, nor do I even try. Why should I beat my head against a brick wall? The more one probes the situation, the more infinite the mystery: it constantly escapes. If mysteries are to preserve their power, they must be respected. *Art is made to disturb: science to reassure.* If there is no mystery,

'Metamorphosis'

there is no poetry, the quality which I hold highest in art. But do not ask me to define it; it is for painting what life is for each man, something which the artist must find for himself through intuition. For me it is a question of harmony, of "relationships", rhythm and above all, the most important element in my work, "metamorphosis". I will explain what I mean by "metamorphosis". For me, no object can be brought back to reality, of whatever nature it may be. A stone may be part of a wall, a sculpture, a mortal weapon, it may be a pebble on a beach or anything else, just as the file which I am holding could be metamorphosed into a shoe horn or a spoon, depending on the way it is used . . . let us give another example. You go to have lunch with a friend, you smell the odour of cooking food and since you are hungry you say to yourself: delicious! But after you have eaten you find the smell of the food which pervades the house, nauseating, and yet it is the same as before. All things change according to circumstance; it is this that I mean by "metamorphosis". When you ask whether a particular form in one of my paintings is the portrait of a female head, a fish, a vase, a bird or all four things together, I cannot give you a categorical answer, because metaphoric confusion is fundamental to poetry. If a form represents different things to different people or many different things together, or outright nothing, it is all the same to me. A form can deal only with the accidental case or with a "rhyme"—a "rhyme" in a painting, in parenthesis,

34

28 *Nu Couchant*
1958, lithograph in colour
$19\frac{1}{2} \times 25\frac{1}{2}$ in (50×65 cm)
Editions Maeght, Paris

can have unexpected consequences, it can change the entire significance of the picture . . . You must understand, I have made a great discovery, I do not believe in anything. Objects only exist for me in as much as they relate to themselves and between themselves and with me. In other words it is not the objects which interest me, but the interaction between them. In fact it is exactly this interaction which is the true subject of my painting. Once this state of harmony has been attained between objects they acquire a quality of intellectual nothingness, which I can only describe as a perfect state of peace and liberty, when everything is possible and just. Life then becomes a continuous revelation. This is true poetry!'[15]

The theme of the sea

Before I move on to the 'fabulous' moment of Braque's *Ateliers,* I would like to touch on a theme, which from the Fauve period, has been a very disquieting one for Braque: the theme of the sea. He has always treated this in a very particular way; for even when the sea is represented in pure colours (up until 1906–7), luminous and almost festive, it was always seen as a disquieting mystery, as a terrifying and monstrous abyss.

In the last period, when Braque lived at Varengeville, facing a sea which no longer contained the warm colours of the South, but a ragged surface, silver, mysterious and treacherous, the theme returns and becomes dominant. It is now terrible and disturbing, like eternal desperation, deserted and yet filled with invisible presence.

It is the period of the *Falaises,* in metallic and sombre colours, the period of the *Marine.* As examples of this see *Barques sur la Plage* 1950 (private collection, Geneva), and *Marine (à la voile déployée)* 1952 (Maeght collection, Paris). In the former the sea is represented by a long, black strip, marked

Pl. 34
Pl. 37

15 Statement by Braque, *The Observer* 1st December 1957 and J. Richardson *op. cit.*

Mirage

Il ne pleut
plus que sur
les arbres...
et sur ma...
tête (la route
est plus écla-

with a white furrow of foam. The beach, in the foreground, is punctuated and variegated, changing from white, to ochre, to light yellow, to green. The sky has come back into existence, a grey-brown, rather like solidified flowing lava, which covers and cancels out the horizon. The boats on the shore are moulds outlined with fleeting strokes. In the second painting the beach, silvered by a suffused, lunar light, is covered by a dark ochre speckled effect; the edge of the beach coincides with the low horizon, while the sea is scarcely visible behind the wavering line of the beach, rolling into dunes. There are some wrecked boats; a strange black and white form looms out of the one on the left (perhaps a sail, or solitary person or a penguin with its gleaming white chest?). One unusual feature in this painting is the distant, tangible sky, lost in the hazy whiteness of an iridescent mist; it is not the usual vertical and enclosing curtain of Braque's skies.

29–32 Four decorated pages from the book by Pierre Reverdy
La Liberté des Mers
1959, lithographs
$22\frac{1}{2} \times 14\frac{1}{2}$ in (57×37 cm)
Editions Maeght, Paris

The 'Atelier' paintings

The marvellous *Ateliers* period extends from 1948 to 1956. All of Braque's concerns at this time, including the appearance of the motif of birds in flight, which were to have such an important influence in graphics and other subsequent work, are reflected in these eight splendid works.

Pl. 35

The first example of an extended development of the birds motif is the ceiling of the Etruscan room at the Louvre. The new quality of liquid space is realised through superimposition of liquid pigment, layer upon layer; these create a heavy, thick crust of sky, standing out on the picture, while the wings of the birds, hewn out, relieve the overall density.

Fig. 23

In the *Ateliers* series all the motifs flow together in unison. (We reproduce No. 5 of the series, or No. 3 according to an alternative enumeration due to the loss of an earlier work, 1949–51, Hänngi collection, Vaduz.) Images of identifiable objects are interwoven with newly invented forms, against a black background; they move in a 'flexible space with varying densities'.[16] It is as if a prophetic wind transforming and lifting everything it touches, is swept by the wings of a giant bird; it starts as an image within the picture (the painting within a painting), but gradually becomes free, as if swimming through a mass of marine flora and fauna.

René Char addresses the painter thus: 'I am delighted by the fact that in the second of the series you have entitled *The Painters' Studio* you have collected and assembled with the ingratitude of a genius, all the greatest elements common to your dream and your work. This wild dove, this phoenix, created like a rapid arrow, whether it flies across the canvas of the open sky of your studio, blows a breath of wind, evokes a presence which overturns all your recent work.'[17]

In this new, fluid, permeable space, objects emerge and dissolve in a kind of 'transubstantiation' rather than 'metamorphosis'. (It is in fact their deepest substance which is changed, not their form.) The range of colours in subtle variations of grey, brown, mauve, ochre, is broken here and there by sudden white flashes. Leymarie writes: 'Their grandiose cadence is that of the organ and oratorio.'[18]

'There was,' as Braque explained, 'a certain silence in the light of my studio.' The theme of birds in flight was, as we have seen, already present; the first sketch for *L'Oiseau et son Nid*, 1956 (Musée National d'Art Moderne, Paris), dates from 1952. None the less, in the last analysis, it was contained in Braque's incessant desire to conquer space; the image of the flying bird is not a symbol for this but rather an enigmatic figurative equivalent, mysteriously breaking the silence with the slow beating of its wings. In *L'Oiseau et son Nid* it is the organic principle of movement. In *A Tire d'Aile*, 1956–61 (Musée National d'Art Moderne, Paris), it becomes an arrow, a splintered fern frond, like a primitive weapon–another example of metamorphosis. Here the same dense mass of liquid blue is broken by an extra-

Pl. 36

Pl. 38

16 J. Leymarie *op. cit.*
17 J. Leymarie *op. cit.*
18 J. Leymarie *op. cit.*

33 Notebook of Georges Braque
1916–47, lithograph
15 × 11 in (38·5 × 28 cm)
Editions Maeght, Paris

ordinary passage: a small panel, on the same scale, reveals another, more naturalistic, bird–a white albatross–slowly flying between two different densities, one as black as shiny metal, the other blue-grey like a dense, suspended atmosphere.

The two-dimensional space of the Cubist period, faceted through super-imposed planes, the tactile space of the still-lifes, the architectonic space of the interiors (*Le Salon, Le Billiard*) has now become 'undulating, dynamic, fluctuating and ethereal. It surpasses all human proportions; it belongs only to the bird in flight'.[19]

In the examples shown here from Braque's graphic work, of which one is reproduced in colour (the poster for his exhibition at the Maeght Gallery in 1956), the theme is almost always the same; the image of space, into which his new conquest, that of movement, is now inserted. Hence the threaded form in the poster, traced in a single stroke on a background of newsprint; the image arbitrates between material conditions and different colours in a unity of pure colour, a clarity of distilled vision, which recalls some of Matisse's last *décollages* (cut-outs) (those for *Jazz,* for example). In the same way, emptiness is now wedged into a thick, uneven, blue surface, dense like a heavy, pleated cloth, as in the Louvre ceiling, poised over a sarcophagus, or in the mural decorations for the villa at Vence, painted about this time.

Clearly, an adequate discussion of Braque's graphics would involve a more extensive treatment. It represents one of the fullest examples of successful expression, of a universe admirably realised, from which one could trace far more links, than in the case of his painting, with so many aspects of contemporary art.

Pl. 40

19 J. Leymaire *op. cit.*

It remains for us to mention briefly Braque's sculpture. This is undoubtedly a painter's sculpture and cannot stand on its own. Even if there are examples of exceptional quality, it is always a painterly quality. They tend to be two-dimensional, expressed on two almost identical sides. The images are, at best, taken in profile and present few substantial differences on either side. They do, however, have a thickness which represents a material weight. In *Hymen,* 1939–57 (Musée d'Art Moderne, Paris), two profiles confront each other, secured below and above by two circular flat shapes, themselves two-dimensional; this motif seems to have been inspired by primitive totems, referring back to the Cubist passion for black African sculpture. *La Tête de Cheval,* 1946–9, bronze (Musée National d'Art Moderne, Paris), is carved as if in a slab, like the earlier reliefs on mythological themes. It is, in the last resort, a beautiful graphic monogram. Finally, we reproduce *La Charrue,* 1955, bronze (Musée National d'Art Moderne, Paris), an elegant double-sided profile, moulded as if by a press.

Braque's sculpture

Pl. 41

Pl. 42

Pl. 43

Art as contemplation

To make a conclusive judgement on Braque's whole work is perhaps not yet possible. We live in a time of uncertainty and evanescent rethinking of ideas. Art itself provides a symptom of the general condition of our society.

Braque, a revolutionary in his approach to pictorial method – that of constant research of ceaseless obsession – gradually renounced, as he left Cubism behind him, most of his own discoveries. He contributed to contemporary art several of the means upon which the revolutionary *avant-garde* was founded: the picture as object which destroyed the idea of the hung painting; the *papier collé,* which, with collage, gave to art a new freedom of means of expression; printed writing on the canvas, which, from Futurism and Cubism onwards, was to have a vast importance in contemporary artistic experiment; research into materials, which gave rise to informality, as an irrational, existential, fact.

Braque continued to pursue his research into materials, yet he never accepted abstraction or informality. This only means that he never renounced painting.

He understood that the tools he himself had offered to the artist would ultimately bring about the destruction of painting as a distinct genre. This would remove painting even further from that which for him was the essential condition of art, that of contemplation. Contemporary art is a form of spying; it defines itself as a receiver of signals as symptomatic of social conditions in a world which tends to be more and more encompassed by the system. Faced with the risk of the destruction of human awareness, faced with organised genocide, one can no longer be permitted the luxury of contemplation. None the less, contemporary art maintains its right to a critical assessment of reality, defining itself as a category of understanding.

The lesson we draw from Braque is therefore valid, both in terms of his attitude and, unequivocally, in terms of quality.

Night and Day: Georges Braque's diaries, 1917–52

Nature does not give a taste for perfection; one does not conceive of it as better or worse.

We will never have rest; the present is eternal.

To think and to reason are two different things.

It is not sufficient that what one paints should be made visible; it must be made tangible.

Emotion cannot grow nor be imitated; it represents the seed, the work of art represents the bud.

In art there can be no effect without a deformation of the truth.

Those who follow: the pure, the whole, the blind, the eunuchs.

I do not do as I wish; I do what I can.

The personality of the artist is not composed by the sum of his fixations.

One cannot ask more of the artist than he can give, nor of the critic more than he can see.

Let us be content to make people reflect; we do not try to convince.

34 *Résurrection de l'Oiseau*
1959, lithograph in colour
16 × 12 in (41 × 31 cm)
Editions Maeght, Paris

Art is made to disturb, science to reassure.

One man says: In the name of God. Another says: God be with us. And a third says: God and my right.

The painter thinks in forms and colours; his object is poetry.

There is no need to imitate what one wants to create.

In art only one thing counts: that which cannot be explained.

If the painter does not despise painting it can be seen in the painting which has more value than himself.

The artist is not unappreciated but misunderstood. People use him without knowing who he is.

Those who walk in front turn their backs on those who follow; that is what followers deserve.

I love rules which correct emotions and emotions that correct rules.

Science is not exempt from insolence; to resolve a problem it is necessary to pose it correctly.

Art soars high; science seeks supports.

It is the precariousness of the work which places the artist in a heroic situation.

When one appeals to talent it means that passion is lacking.

The painter must try not to reconstruct anecdotes, but to construct a pictorial fact.

There is people's art and art for the people, the latter invented by intellectuals. I do not believe that Beethoven or Bach, inspired by popular airs, ever thought of establishing a hierarchy.

When one does not succeed in adapting an existing vocabulary the critics condemn.

35 Lithograph from the book
Le Tir à l'arc
1960, 6 × 8 in (15 × 21 cm)
Editions Maeght, Paris

36 L'Oiseau dans le Feuillage
1961, lithograph
41 × 31½ in (104 × 80 cm)

What concerns me is to achieve a unison with nature rather than to copy her.

To discover something means to strip it naked.

'Climate': one must achieve a certain temperature which makes things malleable.

Pre-classical style is one of rupture; classical style is one of evolution; Mont Saint-Michel and Versailles, Villon and Mme. de Sévigné.

The aspirations of each epoch are limited; hence the illusion of progress.

Common attributes are true, similarities false: Trouillebert resembles Corot, but they have nothing in common.

To write is not to describe; to paint is not to remake.

Realistic representation only deceives.

To each acquisition corresponds a loss; this is the law of compensation.

Limited means generate new forms, invite creation and make for style.

Progress in art does not consist in extending frontiers, but in knowing them better.

I am not a revolutionary painter, I do not seek exaltation: for me fervour is sufficient.

To define something means to substitute for its definition.

To construct means to assemble homogeneous elements; to fabricate means to link them with heterogeneous elements.

Impregnation. Obsession. Hallucination.

When all is said and done I prefer those who exploit me rather than those who follow me: at least they have something to teach me.

Every situation is always complementary to the one that precedes it.

Survival does not abolish memory.

One can divert a river from its course, but not make it climb back to the spring.

Ideas, like clothes, are consumed and deformed by use.

Action is a series of dispersed acts, which allow for the conservation of hope.

37 *Oiseau en Vol*
1961, lithograph
$27\frac{3}{4} \times 23$ in (70·5 × 58·5 cm)
Editions Maeght, Paris

To protect one's illusions, one guards one's words: men today are convinced that they can 'fly' [but *voler,* 'to fly' also means 'to steal'].

Conformism begins with definition.

One cannot always hold one's hat in one's hand; the hat rack was invented for this purpose. I discovered painting so as to hang my ideas from a nail; this allows me to change them and to avoid fixed ideas.

The concept obfuscates the free mind. It was not after great meditation that man drank out of his hand (from the hand to the glass, by way of the shell).

The express train was surmounted by a horse's head.

The container gives form to emptiness, music to silence.

It is a mistake to shut in the unconscious and to place it within the confines of reason.

When the plough is idle it rusts and thus loses its significance.

To have a free mind: to be present.

There are those who would die of thirst between a pitcher of water and a cup of coffee.

Does my theses hold? It is that which you support.

Truth exists; one only invents the nightmare.

One must make a choice: a thing cannot be both true and an exact replica.

With the Renaissance, idealism was substituted for spiritualism.

The future is the projection of the past, conditioned by the present.

I have never been able to distinguish a beginning from an end.

The casual reveals existence.

Mystery is made resplendent by light; mysteriousness is confused with darkness.

Two ideas always exist, one to destroy the other.

To defend an idea means to take a position.

The pessimist does not protect his ideas, he exposes them.

He has changed his mind; like me, he has a nose on his face.

Ideology is construction: a drop of water on these sugar lumps and all dissolves.

Those who depend on the past for prophecy end up ignoring the fact that the past is nothing more than a hypothesis.

The painter recognises things by sight, the writer, who recognises them by name, has the blessing of anticipated judgement. It is for this reason that criticism is easy.

Science is the conquest of the possibility of repetition.

One searches for that which will favour his ideas, the other searches for that which will destroy them.

Truth protects itself: antagonisms grow symetrically around it, never reaching it.

We do not conclude: the present, the fortuitous, will liberate us.

The dictionary is the solid testimonial of an epoch.

It is not the goal which is interesting, but the means used to reach it.

Erudition is knowing without rigour.

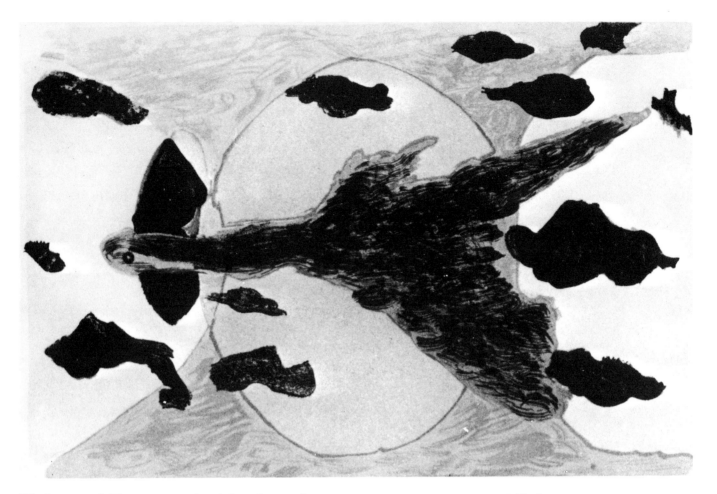

Their excuse? They want to be right where others are wrong.

Hope instead of the ideal. Constancy instead of the habitual. Faith instead of convictions.

Utopia is a myth whose consequences can be foreseen. One makes mistakes.

Democracy has replaced pomp with luxury.

The more socialism is total, the more war will be total.

Idealism is a settled form of hope.

Look for that which is common, not that which is the same. In this way the poet can say: 'a swallow stabs the sky', making the swallow into a dagger.

When we create ideas we move away from truth. If one only has one, it is a fixed idea. One shuts it in.

Magic is not less dangerous for the practitioner than for the victim.

Blood. The cutting steel of the sword.

Fate checkmates ideas. Chance puts them in the street.

The real materialist is the believer.

Spiritualism against idealism. The perpetual against the eternal.

Some, like the naturalist, embalm nature, believing that they can make it immortal.

Magic is the sum of tools which excite credulity.

A still-life ceases to be such when it is no longer within easy reach.

Visual space separates objects one from the other. Tactile space separates itself from objects. The tourist looks at a place. The gunner 'hits' the target (the trajectory is the elongation of the arm).

A unit of tactile measure: the foot, the arm, the thumb.

38 *Equinoxe*
1962, lithograph
$13\frac{3}{4} \times 20\frac{1}{2}$ in ($35 \times 52\cdot5$ cm)
Editions Maeght, Paris

Form and colour do not merge; they are simultaneous.

The painting is finished when it has cancelled the idea.

The idea is the support of the painting.

The subject. A lemon and an adjacent orange cease to be a lemon and orange and become fruit. Mathematics follows this law and so do we.

Few can say, I am here. They look into the past and see into the future.

A memory of 1914: Joffre could not cure himself of having to remake paintings of the battle of Vernet.

That which is not taken, but remains, is the best of us.

Boundaries are the limits of resistance. The lake requires the banks to hold it in.

Reason is a path for the spirit, and a tumult for the soul.

Liberty can be taken but not given. Commonly, liberty means the free exercise of habits; for us it means to surpass the permissible. Liberty is not accessible to all, for many are tied between that which is permitted and that which is prohibited.

Do not ever give in.

For those who indulge in a cult of themselves, convictions substitute faith.

Two things are thought to be similar in terms of one's own second self.

Reason is reasonable.

The echo responds to the echo. Everything rebounds.

Timelessness is the murmuring of a spring.

With age art and life become one.

I do not seek for definition. I move towards infinity.

It is the unpredictable that creates the event.

One thing cannot be in two places at once. One cannot both see it and have it in mind.

The militant man hides behind a mask.

For me the act of painting always remains more important than the result attained.

Culture produces monstrosity.

We must be content to discover but avoid explanation.

Man moves forward as water flows.

In the present nothing is opposed, everything is united. Force and resistance are the same thing.

I avoid my likeness. In every likeness there lies one's second self.

In every reaction there is an element of repentance.

Only he who knows what he wants deceives himself.

I do not protect my ideas, I expose them.

I am subject to sentiments which surpass preference.

There are some works which make the artist think, others which make men think. I have often heard of Manet's talent but never of Cézanne's.

The tooth of a rake.

Cézanne constructed, he did not fabricate; fabrication presupposes an existing framework.

To begin with, the tool was an extension of the arm; with the machine the arm becomes an extension of the tool.

Night, dust, sleep.

Knowledge of the past; revelation of the present.

Visual space. Tactile space. Manual space.

Proof oppresses the truth.

In search of fate one discovers oneself.

One must distinguish between will and constancy. Alcoholism does not represent an example of will.

Fatalism is not, as is often thought, a condition of passivity.

Destroy every idea to attain the inevitable.

Start from the bottom to have some possibility of raising oneself.

From day to day we follow our path.

The drum, instrument of meditation.

He who hears the drum, hears silence.

I desire love as one desires sleep.

Marching towards the star: those before carry the staff, those who follow have the scourge. On the flanks the mass of the rank and file.

Place obstacles in the way of vocations.

They point in a direction, but they take no account of leeway.

Colour plates

1

2

3

4

6

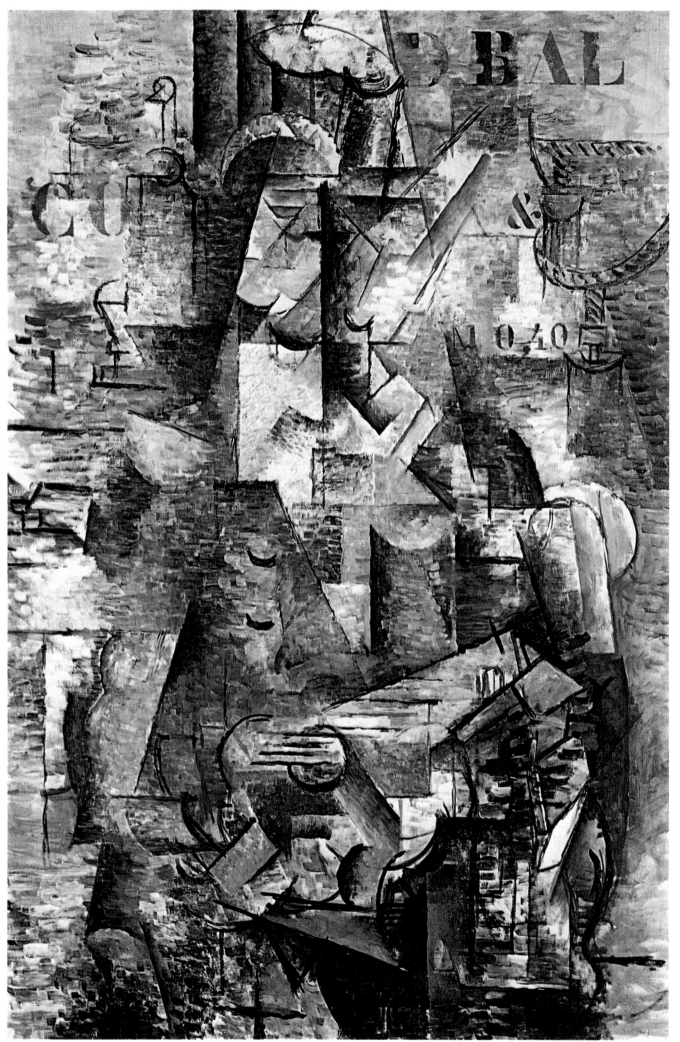

10

12

13

14

15

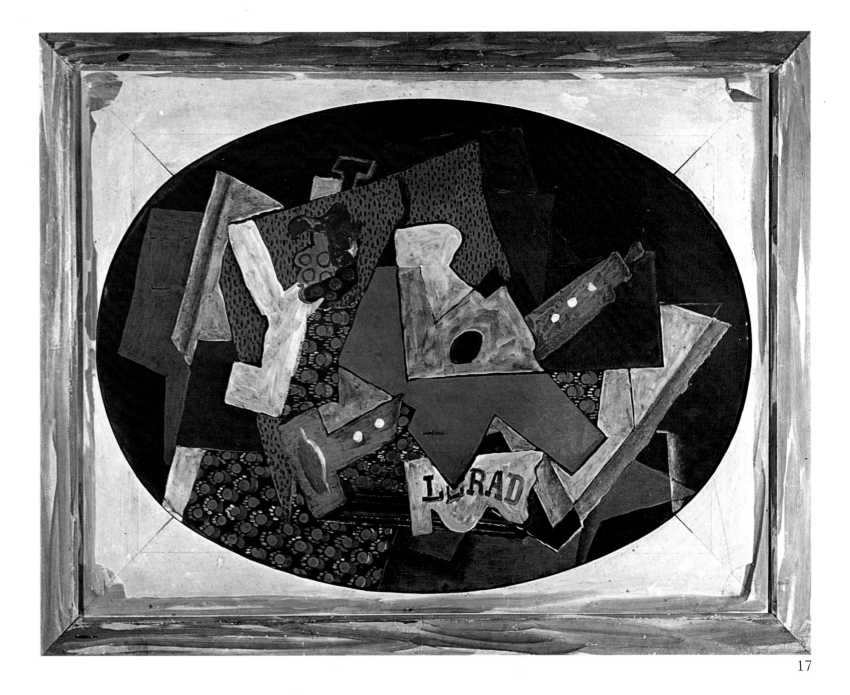

17

18

21

22

23

24

25

26

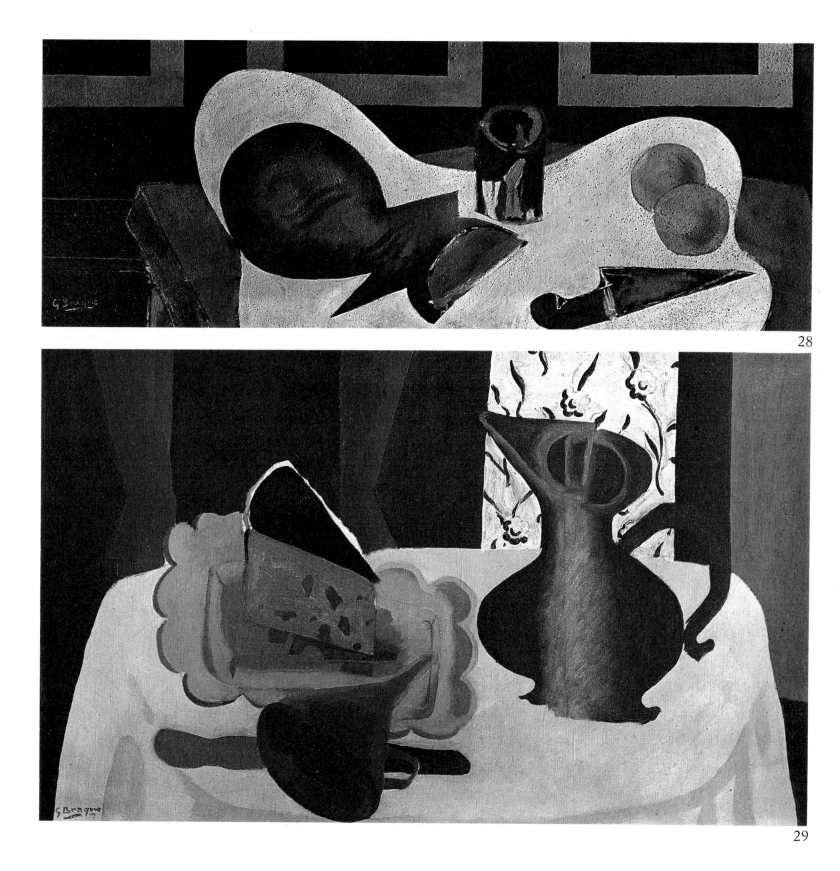

28

29

30

32

34

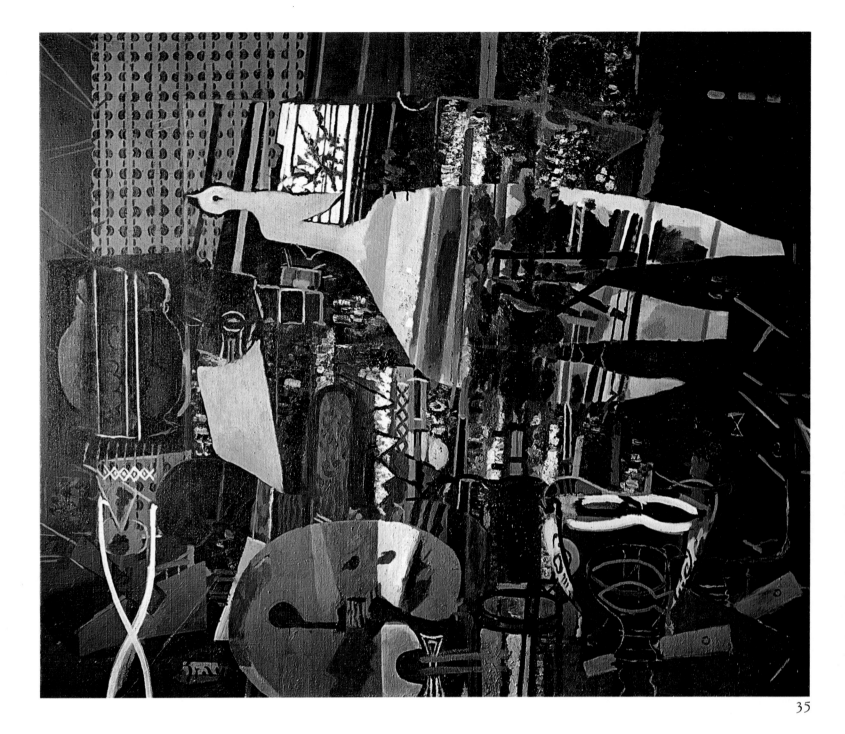

36

39

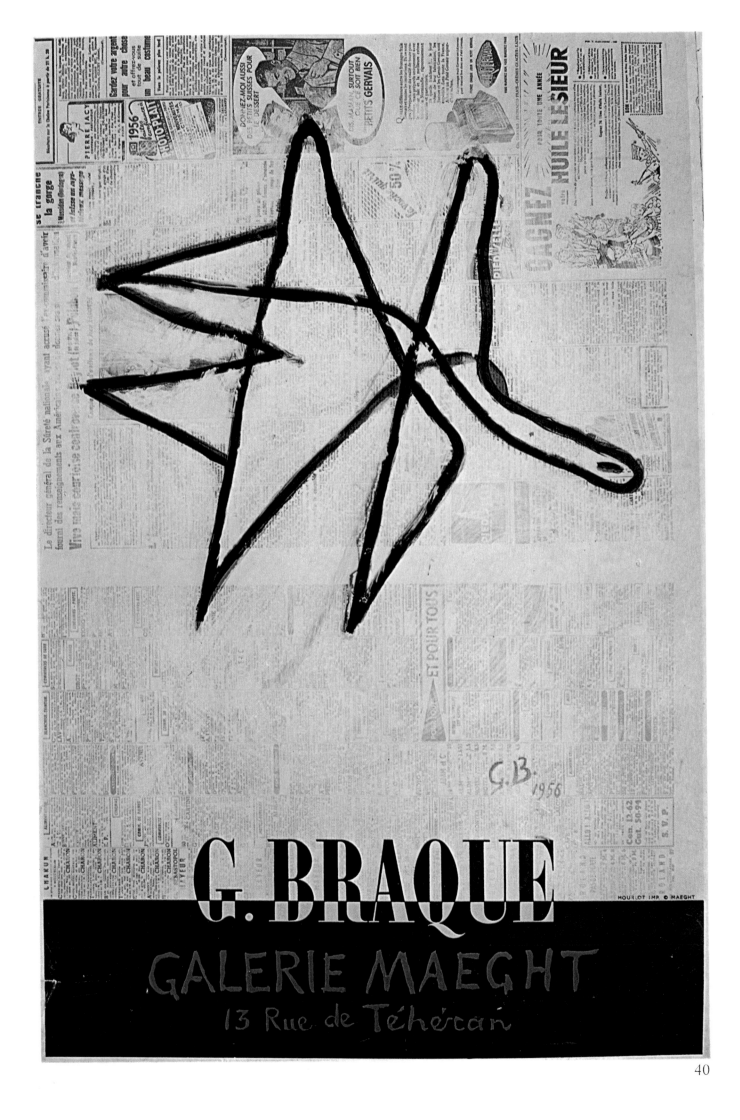

41

42

43

Description of colour plates

1 *Auvers; Les Bateaux Pavoisés*
1905–6, not signed or dated, oil on canvas
20 × 24 in (50·5 × 61·5 cm)
Kunstmuseum, Basle

2 *Le Port de L'Estaque*
1906–7, not signed or dated, oil on canvas
24 × 28¾ in (61 × 73 cm)
Private collection, Zurich

3 *Paysage à L'Estaque*
1908, signed at bottom right 'G. Braque', not dated
oil on canvas 18 × 15 in (46 × 38 cm)
Musée National d'Art Moderne, Paris

4 *Paysage à L'Estaque*
1908, not signed or dated, oil on canvas
32 × 25½ in (81 × 65 cm)
Kunstmuseum, Basle

5 *Violon et Cruche*
1910, not signed or dated, oil on canvas
45¼ × 28¼ in (115 × 72 cm)
Kunstmuseum, Basle

6 *L'Usine du Rio Tinto à L'Estaque*
1910, not signed or dated, oil on canvas
25½ × 20½ in (65 × 52·5 cm)
Musée National d'Art Moderne, Paris

7 *Composition au Violon*
1911, not signed or dated, oil on canvas
50¼ × 34½ in (128 × 88 cm)
Musée National d'Art Moderne, Paris

8 *Le Portugais*
1911, not signed or dated, oil on canvas
45¼ × 31½ in (115 × 80 cm) Kunstmuseum, Basle

9 *Le Guéridon*
1911–12, not signed or dated, oil on canvas
45½ × 32 in (116 × 81 cm)
Musée National d'Art Moderne, Paris

10 *Le Quotidien, Violon et Pipe*
1912, not signed or dated, *papier collé* and oil on canvas
28¼ × 41 in (72 × 104 cm)
Musée National d'Art Moderne, Paris

11 *Composition à l'As de Trèfle*
1912–13, not signed or dated, oil and *papier collé* on canvas
32 × 23 in (81 × 60 cm) Musée National d'Art Moderne, Paris

12 *La Table du Musicien*
1913, not signed or dated, oil and *papier collé* on canvas
25½ × 36 in (65 × 92 cm) Kunstmuseum, Basle

13 *Femme à la Guitare*
1913, not signed or dated, oil and *papier collé* on canvas
53 × 29 in (130·3 × 73·7 cm)
Musée National d'Art Moderne, Paris

14 *Verre et Violon*
1913–14, not signed or dated, oil and *papier collé* on canvas
45½ × 32 in (116 × 82 cm) Kunstmuseum, Basle

15 *Verre, Bouteille et Pipe sur une Table*
1914, not signed or dated, oil and *papier collé* on canvas
18 × 21½ in (46 × 55 cm) Mattioli collection, Milan

16 *La Musicienne*
1917–18, not signed or dated,
mixed technique and *papier collé* on canvas
88 × 42 in (220·5 × 102·5 cm) Kunstmuseum, Basle

17 *Clarinette, Guitare et Compotier*
1918, signed on back 'G. Braque, '18'
mixed technique on canvas
28½ × 39 in (72·5 × 99·5 cm) (oval)
Kunstmuseum, Basle

18 *Nature Morte au Guéridon: Café-Bar*
1919, not signed or dated, oil and sand on canvas
62 × 31½ in (158 × 80 cm) Kunstmuseum, Basle

19 *Bouteille d'Eau de Vie*
1919, not signed or dated, oil and sand on canvas
Kunstmuseum, Basle

20 *Canéphore*
1922, not signed or dated, oil and sand on canvas
71 × 28 in (180 × 72·5 cm)
Musée National d'Art Moderne, Paris

21 *Souvenir de Corot*
1922–3, signed at bottom right, 'G.B.', not dated
oil on canvas 16 × 13 in (41 × 33 cm)
Musée National d'Art Moderne, Paris

22 *Nature Morte aux Poires*
1925, signed at bottom right 'G. Braque'
7½ × 18 in (19 × 46 cm) Musée National d'Art Moderne, Paris

23 *Femme Couchée,*
1930–52, signed at bottom left 'G. Braque'
oil and sand on canvas 28¾ × 71 in (73 × 180 cm)
Musée National d'Art Moderne, Paris

24 *Anémones dans un Vase*
1927, signed at bottom right 'G. Braque, '27'
oil and sand on canvas 18 × 21½ in (46 × 55 cm)
A. M. Roger Varenne collection, Geneva

25 *Grande Nature Morte brune*
1932–3, signed at bottom right 'G. Braque', not dated
oil on canvas 38 × 51 in (97 × 130 cm)
Musée National d'Art Moderne, Paris

26 *Nature Morte à la Pipe*
1932–4, signed at bottom right, 'G. Braque', not dated
oil on canvas 21 × 25½ in (54 × 65 cm)
Kunstmuseum, Basle

27 *Le Guéridon*
1939–52, signed at bottom left 'G. Braque', not dated
oil and sand on canvas 71 × 28¾ in (180 × 73 cm)
Musée National d'Art Moderne, Paris

28 *Le Pain*
1940–1, signed at bottom left 'G. Braque', not dated
oil and sand on canvas 17¾ × 46⅞ in (45 × 119 cm)
George Waechter Memorial Foundation, Geneva

29 *L'Entonnoir*
1914, signed at bottom left 'G. Braque', not dated
oil on canvas 17 × 28¾ in (43·5 × 73 cm)
Musée National d'Art Moderne, Paris

30 *La Table de Toilette*
1942, signed at bottom right 'G. Braque', not dated
oil and sand on canvas 51½ × 38 in (131 × 97 cm)
Musée National d'Art Moderne, Paris

31 *Le Salon*
1944, signed at bottom left 'G. Braque', oil and sand on canvas
59 × 47¼ in (150 × 120 cm)
Musée National d'Art Moderne, Paris

32 *Le Billard*
1945, signed at bottom left 'G. Braque', not dated
oil and sand on canvas 51 × 76¼ in (130 × 194 cm)
Musée National d'Art Moderne, Paris

33 *La Chaise du Jardin*
1948, not signed or dated, oil and sand on canvas
23 × 20 in (59 × 51 cm) Musée National d'Art Moderne, Paris

34 *Barques sur la Plage*
1950, signed at bottom left 'G. Braque', not dated
18 × 24 in (46 × 61 cm) Private collection
Geneva (formerly Crozer Martin collection, Céligny)

35 *Atelier V*
1949–51, signed at bottom left 'G. Braque', not dated
oil and mixed technique on canvas 56½ × 69 in (144 × 175 cm)
Hänngi collection, Vaduz

36 *L'Oiseau et son Nid*
1951–56, signed at bottom left 'G. Braque'
oil and mixed technique on canvas 51 × 68½ in (130 × 173·5 cm)
Musée National d'Art Moderne, Paris

37 *Marine (à la voile déployée)*
1952, signed at bottom left 'G. Braque', not dated
oil and mixed technique on canvas 10¼ × 25¼ in (26 × 64·5 cm)
Maeght collection, Saint-Paul-de-Vence
(formerly Colombe d'Or collection, Vence)

38 *A Tire d'Aile*
1956–61, signed at bottom right 'G. Braque', not dated
mixed technique on canvas 45 × 67 in (115 × 171 cm)
Musée National d'Art Moderne, Paris

39 *L'Oiseau*
1958, signed at bottom right 'G. Braque', oil on canvas
32 × 64 in (82 × 163 cm) Galerie Maeght, Paris

40 *Poster for Braque exhibition*
Exhibition held at the Galerie Maeght in Paris 1956
superimposed image on newsprint 39 × 27½ in (100 × 70 cm)
Galerie Maeght, Paris

41 *Hymen*
1939, bronze, height 30 in (76 cm)
Musée National d'Art Moderne, Paris

42 *La Tête de Cheval*
1946–9, bronze, height 15¾ in (40 cm)
Musée National d'Art Moderne, Paris

43 *La Charrue*
1955, bronze, height 10 in (26 cm)
Musée National d'Art Moderne, Paris

Biographical outline

1882. Born at Argenteuil 13th May.
1890–1900. Lived in Le Havre, attended evening courses at the local Ecole des Beaux-Arts. At seventeen he was employed as an apprentice decorator. Discovered Boudin and Corot at the museum in Le Havre.
1900. Went to Paris to perfect his decorating technique, and attended evening courses in painting and design at the Cours Municipals des Batignolles.
1901. Military service.
1902. Finished his military service and entered the Académie Humbert in Paris, while continuing his technical specialisation. Became friends with Francis Picabia and Marie Laurencin. First paintings of his family. Spent much time at the Louvre, especially in the Egyptian section. In the Durand Ruel and Vollard galleries he discovered the Impressionists: Renoir, Monet, Cézanne, Van Gogh, Seurat.
1903. Admitted to the Ecole des Beaux-Arts, in Léon Bonnat's classes, but after several months returned to the Académie Humbert.
1904. Turned his back on academic teaching and worked by himself in his studio at rue d'Orsel in Montmartre.
1905. Discovered the Fauve painters in the Salon d'Automne, who made a strong impression on him. Became friends with Raoul Dufy and Othon Friesz, whom he had known in Le Havre.
1906. Exhibited seven pictures at the Salon des Indépendants. Went to paint at Anvers with Friesz and adopted the Fauve technique. Spent the winter in L'Estaque.
1907. Exhibited and sold six canvases at the Salon des Indépendants, showed one painting in the Salon d'Automne. Was greatly impressed by the big Cézanne retrospective exhibition. Met Apollinaire who took him to meet Picasso. Became close friends with Picasso—the beginning of a long and important friendship. Saw Picasso's *Les Demoiselles d'Avignon,* which made a strong impression on him. Painted the famous *Grand Nu,* which, with *Les Demoiselles,* was one of the first Cubist paintings.
1908. Under Cézanne's influence, painted canvases of a pre-Cubist nature. His paintings were refused at the Salon d'Automne. In November he held his first one-man show at Galerie Kahnweiler (twenty-seven canvases) presented by Apollinaire.
1909–10. Worked with Derain. The period of Analytical Cubism began.
1911. The first pictures in which letters of the alphabet were used. Spent the summer with Picasso at Ceret (Pyrénées Orientales).
1912. Executed the first *papier-collé.* Married Marcelle Lapre. With Picasso, rented a house at Sorgues (Vaucluse). The phase of Synthetic Cubism began.
1914. First World War. Braque called up.
1915. Seriously wounded at Carency (Artois) and had his skull trepanned.
1916. Fully recovered.
1917. Began work again, interested in the work of Juan Gris and the sculptor Laurens.
1918. Began his series of *Guéridons* (still-life on a round table).
1918. Exhibited at Léonce Rosenberg's Galerie de l'Effort Moderne.
1920. Did his first sculpture.
1922. Received a special invitation to exhibit at the Salon d'Automne (eighteen canvases). Began the series of the *Cheminées.* He settled in Montparnasse, on the avenue Reille.
1923–5. Designed scenes and costumes for Diaghilev's *Ballets Russes (Les Fâcheux,* music by Georges Auric, and *Zéphyre et Flore)* and for Count Etienne de Beaumont *(Salade).*
1924. Exhibited at Galerie Paul Rosenberg. Settled in a house built by Perret, 6 rue du Douanier, where he remained until his death.
1931. Used Greek mythological figures for the first time in his work.
1932. Executed the engravings for Hesiod's *Theogony.*
1933–36. Retrospectives in Basle, London, Brussels.
1937. Received the Carnegie prize.
1939–40. Retrospective in the United States.

1941. Began the series of interiors and still-lifes.
1947. Exhibited for the first time at the Galerie Maeght. Began the large series of *Ateliers*.
1948. Received the *Gran Premio* at the Venice Biennale.
1952-3. Decorated the ceiling of the Etruscan Hall in the Louvre.
1954. Executed a series of windows for the small church at Varengeville where he had gone each summer since 1930. Painted two murals for the villa of Amie Maeght at Saint-Paul-de-Vence.
1956. Large retrospective in Edinburgh and London.
1958. Retrospective in Geneva. Received the Feltrinelli prize in Rome.
1960. Retrospective in Basle. Exhibited all his graphic work at the Bibliothèque Nationale, Paris.
1963. Died on the 31st August in Paris.

39 Photograph of Georges Braque by Man Ray

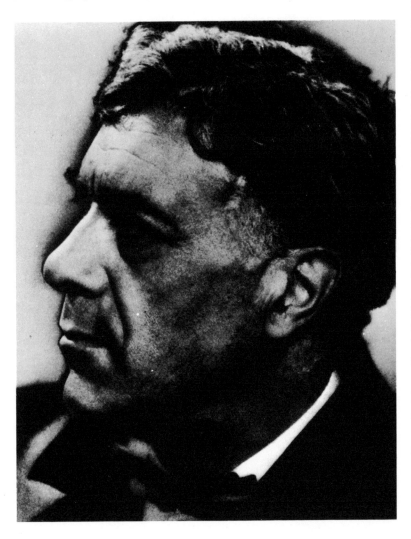

Exhibitions

1906. Salon des Indépendants, Paris (7 works).

1907. Salon d'Automne, Paris (1 work).

1908. 9th–18th November, Galerie Kahnweiler, Paris (27 works; preface to the catalogue by Guillaume Apollinaire).

1909. Salon des Indépendants, Paris (2 works).

1910. Neue Künstlervereinigung, Munich.

1912. Sonderbundausstellung, Cologne; *Zweite Blauer Reiter Ausstellung*, Munich.

1913. February–March, Armory Show, New York, Chicago, Boston (3 works).

1914. 9th December–9th January 1915, Photo Secession Gallery, New York (33 works; with Picasso).

1919. 5th–31st March, Léonce Rosenberg's Galerie de l'Effort Moderne, Paris.

1920. Salon d'Automne, Paris (3 works); Salon des Indépendants, Paris (3 works).

1921. 30th May, Hôtel Druot, Paris (17 works) sold by Uhde; 13th–14th June, first section, Hôtel Druot, Paris (22 works) sold by Kahnweiler; 17th–18th November, second section, Hôtel Druot, Paris (38 works) sold by Kahnweiler.

1922. 4th July, third section, Hôtel Druot, Paris (18 works) sold by Kahnweiler.

1923. 7th May, fourth section, Hôtel Druot, Paris (35 works) sold by Kahnweiler.

1924. 2nd–21st May, Galerie Paul Rosenberg, Paris (62 works).

1925. March, Galerie Flechtheim, Berlin; December, Galerie Vavin-Raspail, Paris.

1926. 8th–27th March, Galerie Paul Rosenberg, Paris (62 works).

1929. May, Galerie Paul Rosenberg, Paris.

1930. May, Galerie Paul Rosenberg, Paris; June–July, *Cent Ans de Peinture Française* Galerie Georges Petit, Paris; 21st September–15th October, Matisse, Braque, Picasso, Galerie Flechtheim, Berlin (24 works).

1931. February, *Picasso, Braque, Léger*, Museum of French Art, New York (catalogue preface by Maud Dale).

1933. 9th April–14th May, *Braque*, Kunsthalle, Basle (183 works, catalogue preface by Carl Einstein).

1934. 13th–31st March, *Braque, Matisse, Picasso*, Gallery Durand-Ruel, New York (13 works); July, Alex Reid and Léfèvre Galleries, London (41 works); 26th November–15th December, *Œuvres Récentes*, Valentine Gallery, New York (16 works).

1935. March–April, *Les Créateurs du Cubisme*, Galerie des Beaux-Arts, Paris (25 works; catalogue preface by Maurice Raynal, text by Raymond Cogniat); 23rd April, Hôtel Druot, Paris (16 works) sold by Jacques Zoubaboff.

1936. 8th–31st January, *Œuvres Récentes*, Galerie Paul Rosenberg, Paris (20 works); July, Alex Reid and Léfèvre Galleries, London (41 works); 2nd March–19th April, *Cubism and Abstract Art*, Museum of Modern Art, New York (9 works); November–December, Palais des Beaux-Arts, Brussels (81 works); The 1936 International Exhibition of Paintings, Carnegie Institute, Pittsburgh (and award to Braque).

1937. 6th–30th January, *Matisse, Braque, Picasso*, Galerie Paul Rosenberg, Paris (20 works); 3rd–30th April, *Œuvres Récentes*, Galerie Paul Rosenberg, Paris (18 works); June–October, *Maîtres de l'Art Indépendant (1895–37)*, Musée Municipal d'Art Moderne, Petit Palais, Paris (25 works); Carnegie Institute, Pittsburgh.

1938. 4th–21st February, *L'Epoque Fauve de Braque 1906*, Galerie Pierre, Paris (20 works), 14th–25th October, Buchholz Gallery, New York (16 works); 16th November–10th December, Galerie Paul Rosenberg, Paris (22 works); *Matisse, Picasso, Braque, Laurens*, Stockholm, Oslo, Copenhagen, and Göteborg (39 works; catalogue text by Walter Halvorsen).

1939. 4th–29th April, Galerie Paul Rosenberg, Paris (27 works); 6th June–8th July, *Œuvres Récentes*, Galerie Paul Rosenberg, Paris; Helft Gallery, London (24 works); 7th–27th November, *Retrospective*, Arts Club of Chicago (68 works; catalogue preface by J. Johnson Sweeney); 6th December–6th January 1940, *Retrospective*, Duncan Phillips Memorial Gallery, Washington, and San Francisco (55 works; catalogue texts by Duncan Phillips, Henry McBride, J. Johnson Sweeney).

1940. 6th February–3rd March, *Retrospective*, Museum of Art, San Francisco (67 works); A. E. Gallatin collection, New York and Philadelphia Museum (11 works); same at Philadelphia Museum (catalogue notes by L. H. Morris; introduction by Jean Hélion).

1941. 6th January–4th March, Chrysler Collection, Virginia Museum of Fine Arts, Richmond and Philadelphia (15 works); 13th January–8th February, Valentine Gallery, New York (27 works).

1942. 7th–25th April, Galerie Paul Rosenberg, New York (13 works); 22nd November–27th December, Museum of Art, Baltimore (16 works).

1943. 6th April–1st May. *Braque and Picasso*, Galerie Paul Rosenberg, New York, (6 works); 25th September–31st October, Salon d'Automne, Paris (35 works).

1944. 6th October–5th November, Salon d'Automne, Paris (2 works); 6th November–2nd December, *Braque, Matisse, Picasso*, Galerie Paul Rosenberg, New York (4 works by Braque).

1945. 15th April–15th May, *Les Emaux de Ligugé*, Galerie de France, Paris (8 pieces in enamelled copper); 24th May–30th June, *Le Cubisme, 1911–1918*, Galerie de France, Paris (9 works; catalogue preface by Bernard Dorival, notes by André Lhote); June–November, *Braque, Picasso, Léger*, Museum of Modern Art, Philadelphia (9 works by Braque); 20th October–12th November, Stedelijk Museum, Amsterdam (26 works); 24th November–13th December, Palais des Beaux-Arts, Brussels (27 works).

1946. April, *Exposition d'Art sacré*, Galerie René Drouin (1 work; catalogue and preface by Morel); 28th April–18th May, Galerie Paul Rosenberg, New York (11 works); May, *Braque, Rouault*, Tate Gallery, London (28 works, catalogue introduction by Germaine Bazin); 28th June–30th September, *Braque, Picasso*, Art Institute, Chicago (5 works); 21st September–20th October, *Braque, Kandinsky, Picasso*, Kunsthaus, Zurich (26 works).

1947. June, Galerie Maeght, Paris (58 works; catalogue text by René Char, Georges Braque, Jacques Kober); 27th June–30th September, *Peintures et Sculptures contemporaines*, Palais des Papes, Avignon (13 works); November, Galerie Seligmann-Helft, New York.

1948. 5th–24th January, Galerie Paul Rosenberg, New York (15 works); 26th February–24th March, *Braque, Picasso, Gris*, Kunsthalle, Basle (40 works); 2nd–29th April, Kunsthalle, Bern (37 works); June, *Œuvres Graphiques*, Galerie Maeght, Paris; May–October, Venice Biennale (18 works; Gran Premio); July, *Œuvres Graphiques*, Galleria del Cavallino, Milan; September, Athénée, Geneva; October, Gallery of Modern Art, Basle.

1948. Spring, Museum of Modern Art, New York, and Cleveland (115 works; catalogue introduction by Jean Cassou); *Georges Braque: Gemälde, Graphic, Plastik*, Stuttgart.

1950. 29th April–29th May, *Les Fauves*, Kunsthalle, Bern (11 works); September, *Braque*, Samlaren Gallery, Stockholm (56 works); 13th November–23rd December, *Les Fauves*, Sidney Janis Galery, New York (4 works); *Georges Braque: Das Graphische Werk*, Buchheim, Feldafing, Germany (catalogue text by Lothar-Gunther Buchheim).

1951. *Sur quatres murs*, Galerie Maeght, Paris (catalogue text by Pierre Reverdy); June–September, *Le Fauvisme*, Musée National d'Art Moderne, Paris (11 works); *La Nature Morte Française du XVIIe siècle à nos jours*, Galerie Charpentier, Paris (3 works).

1952. April–September, *La Nature Morte de l'Antiquité à nos Jours*, Musée de l'Orangerie, Paris (2 works; catalogue by Charles Sterling); June–July, *Georges Braque*, Galerie Maeght, Paris (41 works; catalogue and text by A. Giacometti and J. Grenier); March–April, *Cinquante Ans de Peinture Française dans les Collections Particulières: Cézanne à Matisse*, Musée des Arts Décoratifs, Paris (7 works); *Braque* Exhibition in Tokyo; May–June, *L'œuvre du XXe siècle*, Musée National d'Art Moderne, Paris (5 works).

1953. 30th January–9th April, *Le Cubisme 1907–14*, Musée National d'Art Moderne, Paris (catalogue introduction by Jean Cassou; chronology by Bernard Dorival); 25th April–31st May, *Braque*, Kunsthalle, Bern (157 works; catalogue preface by A. Rudingler); 14th November–6th December, *L'Œuvre Graphique de Braque*, Musée des Beaux-Arts, Liège (96 works; catalogue and text by Michel Seuphor); 20th November–15th December, *Sculptures by Painters*, Valentine Gallery, New York (6 works).

1954. 14th May–3rd July, *Braque, Paintings and Drawings from Collections in England, with Lithographs 1909–53*, ICA Gallery, London; December–January 1955, *La Théogonie d'Hésiode et de Braque*, Galerie Maeght, Paris (catalogue preface by Georges Limbour); *Dessins de Toulouse-Lautrec aux Cubistes*, Musée National d'Art Moderne, Paris (9 works; catalogue by Bernard Dorival).

1955. January–July, *Braque, Das Graphische Gesamtwerk, 1907–55*; Cologne, Bremen, Düsseldorf, Krefeld, Berlin (59 works and 10 illustrated books; catalogue preface by Paul Wember); 31st May–5th September, *Paintings from Private Collections*, Museum of Modern Art, New York (5 works).

1956. February–April, *La Collection Hermann Rupf*, Kunstmuseum, Bern (10 works); May–June, *Toiles récentes de Georges Braque*, Galerie Maeght, Paris; *Braque Retrospective* at the Scottish Royal Academy, Edinburgh, the Tate Gallery, London, and the Boymans Museum, Rotterdam.

1958. Galerie Maeght, Paris; Retrospective at the Athénée, Geneva; Palazzo Barberini, Rome; Venice Biennale.

1959. Galerie Maeght, Paris.

1960. *Œuvre Graphique*, Bibliothèque Nationale, Paris; Retrospective at the Kunsthalle, Basle.

1961. *L'Atelier de Braque*, Musée du Louvre, Paris.

1962. Contemporary Art Center, Cincinatti; 23rd March–6th May, Museum für Kunst und Gewerbe, Hamburg (with Chagall and Miró; catalogue and presentation by Lieselotte Möller).

1963. Galerie Maeght, Paris; Haus der Kunst, Munich.

Bibliography

WRITINGS OF GEORGES BRAQUE

'Pensées et Réflexions sur la Peinture' in *Nord-Sud*, No. 10, Paris, December 1917; G. JEDLICKA, 'Begegnung mit G. Braque' in *Begegnungen*, Basle, 1933; 'Réponse à une enquête' in *Cahiers d'Art*, No. 14, 1939; G. DIEHL, 'L'univers pictural et son destin' (interview with Braque) in *Problèmes de la peinture*, Paris, 1945; 'Réponse à une Enquête de G. Braque' in *Lettres françaises*, March 1946; *Cahiers de G. Braque 1917–47*, Paris, 1948, with supplement 1947–56, Paris, 1956, current edition entitled *Le jour et la nuit, 1917–52*, Paris, 1952; A. IMAIZUMI, 'Conversation with Braque' in *Misue*, Tokyo, October 1952; W. TERIADE, 'Braque parle' in *Verve*, No. 27–28, 1952; G. RIBEMONT-DESSAIGNE, 'Braque: L'Abstrait c'est de la peinture mondaine' in *Arts*, September 1953; 'Braque: La Peinture et nous: Propos de l'artiste recueillis par DORA VALLIER' in *Cahiers d'Art*, No. 1, 1954; J. RICHARDSON, 'The Thoughts of Braque' in *The Observer*, 1st December 1957; G. CHARBONNIER, 'Braque' in *Le Monologue du Peintre*, Paris, 1959.

BOOKS AND MONOGRAPHS

G. APOLLINAIRE, Preface to the catalogue of Braque's exhibition at the Galerie Kahnweiler, Paris, 1908; M. DENIS, *Théories*, Paris, 1912; A. GLEIZES, J. METZINGER, *Du Cubisme*, Paris, 1912; A. SALMON, *La jeune peinture française*, Paris, 1912; G. APOLLINAIRE, *Les peintres cubistes*, Paris, 1913, new edition, Geneva, 1950; J. GORDON, *Modern French Painters*, New York, 1913, London, 1923; J. N. LAURVIC, *Is it Art? Post-Impressionism, Cubism and Futurism*, New York, 1913; A. J. EDDY, *Cubism and Post-Impressionism*, Chicago, 1914; A. SOFFICI, *Cubismo e futurismo*, Florence, 1914; G. COQUIOT, *Cubistes, futuristes, passéistes*, Paris, 1914; W. HUNTINGTON WRIGHT, *Modern Painting, Its Tendencies and Meaning*, New York, 1915; S. KIMURA, *The Arts of Futurism and Cubism*, Tokyo, 1915; T. DÄUBLER, *Der neue Standpunkt*, Dresden, 1916; H. WALDEN, *Einblick in Kunst: Expressionismus, Futurismus, Kubismus*, Berlin, 1917; R. ALLARD, *Le nouveau spectateur*, Paris, 1919–21; T. DÄUBLER, *Im Kampf um die Moderne Kunst*, Berlin, 1919; M. RAYNAL, *Quelques intentions du Cubisme*, Paris, 1919; O. GRAUTOFF, *Formzertrümmerung und Formaufbau in der bildenden Kunst*, Berlin, 1919; R. BISSIÈRE, *Georges Braque*, Paris, 1920; A. GLEIZES, *Du Cubisme et des moyens de le comprendre*, Paris, 1920; D. HENRY (KAHNWEILER), *Der Weg zum Kubismus*, Munich, 1920; P. E. KUPPERS, *Der Kubismus*, Leipzig, 1920; L. ROSENBERG, *Cubisme et tradition*, Paris, 1920; A. SALMON, *L'Art vivant*, Paris, 1920; R. BLUMMER, *Der Geist des Kubismus und die Künste*, Berlin, 1921; L. ROSENBERG, *Cubisme et empirisme*, Paris, 1921; G. SEVERINI, *Du Cubisme au classicisme*, Paris, 1921; M. DENIS, *Nouvelles théories*, Paris, 1922; P. F. SCHMIDT, *Die Kunst der Gegenwart*, Berlin, 1922; M. RAYNAL, *Braque*, Paris, 1923, Rome, 1924; H. KRÖLLER-MÜLLER, *Die Entwicklung der modernen Malerei*, Leipzig, 1925; A. OZENFANT and C. E. JEANNERET, *Le peinture moderne*, Paris, 1925; C. PAVOLINI, *Cubismo, Futurismo, Espressionismo*, Bologna, 1926; C. EINSTEIN, *Die Kunst des 20. Jahrhunderts*, Berlin, 1926 and 1931; P. COURTHION, *Panorama de la peinture française*, Paris, 1927; K. MALEVITČ, *Die Gegenstandlose Welt*, Munich, 1927; M. RAYNAL, *Anthologie de la Peinture en France*, Paris, 1927; A. WILENSKIJ, *The Modern Movement in Art*, London, 1927; A. BRETON, *Le Surréalisme et la Peinture*, Paris, 1928; P. GUILLAUME, *L'Art Cubiste*, Paris, 1929; G. JANNEAU, *L'Art Cubiste*, Paris, 1929; R. HUYGHE, *Georges Braque*, Paris, 1932; G. ISARLOV, *Georges Braque*, Paris, 1932; J. HELION, *Evolution of Abstract Art*, New York, 1933; H. READ, *Art Now*, London, 1933 and 1948; F. OLIVIER, *Picasso et ses amis*, Paris, 1933 and 1955; C. EINSTEIN, *Georges Braque*, Paris, 1934; G. JEDLICKA, *Georges Braque*, Paris, 1934; R. HUYGHE, *Histoire de l'art contemporain*, Paris, 1935; A. H. BARR Jr, *Cubism and Abstract Art*, New York, 1936; C. J. BULLIET, *The Significant Moderns and their Pictures*, New York, 1936; C. ZERVOS, *Histoire de l'art contemporain*, Paris, 1938; R. HUYGHE, *Les Contemporains*, Paris, 1939; A. E. GALLATIN, *Museum of Living Art*, New York, 1940 (notes by L. H. Morris, introduction by J. Hélion); S. FUMET, *Braque*, Paris, 1941; G. DIEHL, *Les Fauves*, Paris, 1943; B. DORIVAL, *Les étapes de la peinture française contemporaine*, Paris, 1943–4; A. E. GALLATIN, *Georges Braque*, New York, 1943; B. DORIVAL, *Le Fauvisme et le Cubisme 1905–1911*, Vol. I, Paris, 1944; E. BILLE, *Picasso, Surrealism, Abstract Art*, Copenhagen, 1945; E. BONFANTE, J. RAVENNA, *Georges Braque, Arte Cubista*, Venice, 1945; B. DORIVAL, *Le Cubisme, 1911–1918* (catalogue of the exhibition at the Galerie de France), Vol. II, Paris, 1945; S. FUMET, *Braque*, Mulhouse, Paris, London and New York, 1945; J. PAULHAN, *Braque le patron*, Paris, 1945 and 1952, Geneva, 1946; L. VENTURI, *Painting and Painters*, New York, 1945; D. WALLARD, *Braque*, Paris, 1945; F. PONGE, *Braque le Réconciliateur*, Geneva, 1946; L. MOHOLY-NAGY, *Space-Time Problems in Art*, New York, 1946; *Anthologie du livre illustré par les peintres de l'école de Paris*, Geneva, 1946; M. RAYNAL, *Peintres du XXe siècle*, Geneva, 1947; G. C. ARGAN, *Il Cubismo*, 1948, reprinted in *Studi e note*, Rome, 1955; D. Cooper, *Braque: Paintings 1909–1947*, London, 1948; V. CRASTRE, *La naissance du Cubisme*, Geneva, 1948; J. GRENIER, *Braque: Peintures 1942–1947*, Paris, 1948; J. GRENIER, *Peintures de Braque 1909–1947*, Paris, 1948; E. AZCOAGA, *El Cubismo*, Barcelona, 1948; F. PONGE, *Le Peintre à l'étude*, Paris, 1948; G. DUTHUIT, *Les Fauves*, Geneva, 1949; E. GAUSS, *Aesthetic Theories of French Artists*, Baltimore, 1949; H. R. HOPE, *Georges Braque*, New York, 1949; D. H. KAHNWEILER, *The Rise of Cubism*, New York, 1949; A. LEJARD, *Braque*, Paris, 1949; P. REVERDY, *Braque: une aventure méthodique*, Paris, 1949; M. SEUPHOR, *L'Art abstrait*, Paris, 1949; D. H. KAHNWEILER, *Les années héroiques du Cubisme*, Paris, 1950; F. PONGE, *Braque: Dessins*, Paris, 1950; M. RAYNAL, *Histoire de la Peinture moderne*, Geneva, 1950; P. FRANCASTEL, *Peinture et société*, Lyons, 1951; S. FUMET, *Sculptures de Georges Braque*, Paris, 1951; L. VENTURI, 'Premesse teoriche dell'arte moderna' in *Problemi attuali di scienza e di cultura* No. 24, 1951, reprinted in *Saggie Critica*, Rome, 1956; L. G. BUCHHEIM, *Georges Braque: Das Graphische Werk*, 1952; C. STERLING, *La Nature morte de l'Antiquité à nos jours*, Paris, 1952 and 1959; J. LASSAIGNE, *Painters of the Twentieth Century: Cubism and Fantastic Art*, Geneva, 1952; A. E. GALLATIN, *Georges Braque*, New York, 1953; C. GRAY, *Cubist Aesthetic Theories*, Baltimore, 1953; M. RAYNAL, *La peinture moderne*, Geneva, 1953; M. SEUPHOR, *L'œuvre graphique de Braque*, Paris, 1953; *Le Cubisme 1907–1914* (catalogue of the exhibition at the Musée National d'Art Moderne), Paris, 1953; A. H. BARR Jr, *Masters of Modern Art*, New York, 1954; W. HAFTMANN, *Malerei im 20. Jahrhundert*, Munich, 1954; F. LAUFER, *Georges Braque*, Bern, 1954; F. ELGAR (ed.), *Dictionnaire de la peinture moderne*, Paris, 1954; P. FRANCASTEL, *La Peinture française du classicisme au cubisme*, Paris, 1955; R. GENAILLE, *La Peinture contemporaine*, Paris, 1955; P. HERON, *The Changing Form of Art*, London, 1955; *Histoire de la peinture moderne*, Vol. III, Geneva, 1955; J. CASSOU, *Braque*, Paris, 1956; D. COOPER, *Letters of Juan Gris*, London, 1956; P. DESCARGUES, *Le Cubisme*, Paris, 1956; F. FOSCA, *Bilan du Cubisme*, Paris, 1956; M. GIEURE, *Georges Braque*, Paris, 1956; M. GIEURE, *Braque: Dessins*, Paris, 1956; G. SCHMIDT, *Petite histoire de la peinture moderne*, Neuchâtel, 1956; A. VERDET, *Georges Braque*, Geneva and Munich, 1956; P. HERON, *Braque*, London, 1957; G. C. ARGAN, *Braque*, New York, Amsterdam and Milan, 1957; R. DELAUNAY, *Du Cubisme à l'art abstrait*, Paris, 1957; B. DORIVAL, *Peintres du XXᵉ siècle*, Paris, 1957; E. ENGELBERTS, *Georges Braque: œuvre graphique original*, Geneva, 1958; J. GOLDING, *Cubism: A History and an Analysis 1907–1914*, London, 1959; J. GRENIER, *Essais sur la peinture contemporaine*, Paris, 1959; G. HABASQUE, *Cubism: Biographical and Critical Studies*, Paris and New York, 1959; G. HABASQUE, *Le Cubisme*, Geneva, 1959; J. LEYMARIE, *Le Fauvisme*, Geneva, 1959; J. RUSSELL, *Georges Braque*, London, 1959; A. VERDET, *Braque le solitaire*, Paris, 1959; CAIN, VALERY and RADET, *Georges Braque, œuvre graphique, Bibliothèque Nationale*, Paris, 1960; J. CASSOU, *Panorama des arts plastiques contemporains*, Paris, 1960; C. ZERVOS, *Georges Braque, nouvelles sculptures et plaques gravées*, Paris, 1960; G. APOLLINAIRE, *Chroniques d'art 1908–18*, Paris, 1960; J. CASSOU, *L'atelier de Braque*, Paris, 1961; W. HOFMANN, *L'œuvre graphique de Georges Braque*, Stuttgart and Lausanne, 1961; J. LEYMARIE, *Braque*, Geneva, 1961; G. C. ARGAN, *Scienza e artigianato di Braque*, 1962, reprinted in *Salvezza e caduta dell' Arte moderna*, Milan, 1964; J. RICHARDSON, *Braque*, Milan, 1961 and London, 1962; R. ROSENBLUM, *Cubism and Twentieth Century Art*, New York, 1961; E. ENGELBERTS, *L'Œuvre graphique de Georges Braque* (introduction by W. HOFMANN), Lausanne, 1962; R. ROSENBLUM, *La storia del Cubismo e l'arte del ventesimo secolo*, Milan, 1962; P. CABANNE, *L'épopée du Cubisme*, Paris, 1963; D. COOPER, Preface to the catalogue of the Braque exhibition in the Haus der Kunst, Munich, 1963; J. GOLDING, *Storia del Cubismo*, Turin, 1963; MOURIOT, *Braque lithographe*, Monte Carlo, 1963; U. APOLLONIO, *Braque*, Milan, 1965; J. CASSOU, 'Introduction' in *Georges Braque, Présentation de la Donation Braque au Musée du Louvre*, Paris, 1965; E. FRY, *Cubism*, New York, 1966; N. WADLEY, *Cubism*, London, 1970.

ARTICLES FROM PERIODICALS

L. VAUXCELLES, *Gil Blas*, 10th March and 14th November 1908, 25th March 1909; G. APOLLINAIRE, *Le Mercure de France*, 16th January 1909; L. VAUXCELLES, *Le Télégramme*, 5th January 1909; S. MAKOVSKI, *Apollon*, No. 10, 1910; A. SOFFICI, 'Picasso e Braque' in *La Voce*, Florence, 24th August 1911; G. APOLLINAIRE, *L'esprit nouveau et les poètes* in *Le Mercure de France*, 2nd December 1918; A. LHOTE, 'Braque' in *La Nouvelle Revue Française*, 1st June 1919; B. CENDRARS, *La rose rouge*, June 1919; H. HERTZ, 'Braque et le reveil des apparences' in *L'Amour de l'Art*, Paris, 1926; E. TERIADE, 'Les dessins de Georges Braque' in *Cahiers d'Art*, No. 2, 1927; C. ZERVOS, 'Georges Braque et la peinture française' in *Cahiers d'Art*, No. 2, 1927; J. CASSOU, 'Georges Braque' in *Cahiers d'Art*, No. 1, 1928; E. TERIADE, 'L'épanouissement de l'œuvre de Braque' in *Cahiers d'Art*, No. 1, 1928; C. EINSTEIN, 'Tableaux récents de Georges Braque' in *Documents*, 1929; W. GROHMANN, 'Georges Braque' in *Cicerone*, 1929; E. BOVE, 'Georges Braque' in *Formes*, March 1930; C. ZERVOS, 'Observations sur les peintures récentes de Georges Braque' in *Cahiers d'Art*, No. 5, 1930; F. OLIVIER, 'La naissance de Cubisme' in *Le Mercure de France*, 15th June 1931; R. COGNIAT, 'Braque et les ballets russes' in *L'Amour de l'Art*, May 1931; C. ZERVOS, 'Le classicisme de Braque' in *Cahiers d'Art*, No. 6, 1931; C. ZERVOS, 'Georges Braque et le développement du Cubisme' in *Cahiers d'Art*, No. 7, 1932; J. CASSOU, *L'Amour de l'Art*, No. 14, November 1933; R. HUYGHE, *L'Amour de l'Art*, No. 14, November 1933; A. LHOTE, 'Les créateurs du Cubisme' in *La Nouvelle Revue Française*, 1st May 1935; A. LHOTE, 'Le symbolisme plastique de Georges Braque' in *La Nouvelle Revue Française*, No. 48, 1937; B. BRANDT, 'Photographies de Georges Braque' in *Verre*, No. 2, Spring 1938; E. KALLAI, 'Georges Braque' in *Magyar Müvészat*, No. 14, Budapest, October 1938; G. BAZIN, 'Braque' in *Prométhée*, No. 20, 1939; C. ZERVOS, 'Braque et la Grèce primitive' in *Cahiers d'Art*, No. 22, 1940; J. BABELON, 'Braque et la nature morte' in *Beaux-Arts*, 30th September 1943; J. PAULHAN, 'Braque ou le sens du caché' in *Cahiers d'Art*, 1940–44; G. BAZIN, 'Braque' in *Labyrinthe*, 15th January, 1945; J. AMBLER, 'The Gallic Traditionalism of Braque' in *Bulletin of the City Art Museum*, Saint Louis, April 1945; J. PAULHAN, 'Braque le patron' in *Horizon*, No. 65, 1945 and in *Poésies*, No. 43, 1945; J. BRASSAI, 'Photographies de Braque dans son atelier' in *Harper's Bazaar*, No. 3, 1946; J. CASSOU, 'Le secret de Braque' in *L'Amour de l'Art*, January 1946; A. JAKOWSKI, 'Georges Braque' in *Art de France*, No. 8, 1946; J. GRENIER, 'Introduction à la peinture de Georges Braque' in *Variété*, No. 3, 1946; F. PONGE, 'Braque le Réconciliateur' in *Labyrinthe*, 23rd December 1946; A. WARNOD, 'Georges Braque s'est remis au travail' in *Arts*, February 1946; R. DUVAL, 'Photographies de Braque' in *L'Amour de l'Art*, No. 5, 1947; G. VERONESI, 'Braque, Picasso, Calder' in *Emporium*, November–December 1947; C. ZERVOS, 'Œuvres de Braque' in *Cahiers d'Art*, No. 22, 1947; G. ROSENTHAL, 'The Art of

Braque' in *Baltimore Museum of Art News*, April 1948; W. O. JUDKINS, 'Toward a Reinterpretation of Cubism' in *Art Bulletin*, No. 34, 1948; M. ZAHAR, 'L'orientation de Georges Braque' in *Panorama des Arts*, 1948; A. M. FRANKFURTER, 'Georges Braque' in *Art News*, February 1949; M. ARLAND, 'Braque' in *L'age nouveau*, No. 42, 1949; P. M. LAPORTE, 'Cubism and Science' in *Journal of Aesthetics and Art Criticism*, 1949; L. DEGAND, 'Braque' in *Art d'Aujourd'hui*, No. 7–8, 1950; J. BOURET, 'Braque ou l'andante noir et gris' in *Arts*, 17th February 1950; C. ZERVOS, 'Georges Braque' in *Cahiers d'Art*, No. 26, 1951; R. DE SOLIER, 'L'œuvre gravé de Braque' in *Cahiers de la Pléiade*, No. 12, 1951; R. CHAR, 'Georges Braque' in *Cahiers d'Art*, 1951; H. CHADET and H. DE SEGONZAC, 'Georges Braque, le "père tranquille" du Cubisme' in *Paris Match*, No. 271, 5th June 1952; P. M. GRAND, 'Céramiques de peintres' in *Art et Décoration*, No. 32, 1952; G. BAZIN, 'Sur l'espace en peinture: la vision de Braque' in *Journal de Psychologie*, No. 45, 1953; P. C., 'Le plafond de Braque au Louvre' in *Journal de l'Amateur d'Art*, 10th May 1953; P. LIMBOURG, 'Braque a pensé "plafond"' in *Journal de l'Amateur d'art*, 10th June 1953; G. RIBEMONT-DESSAIGNES, 'Georges Braque dit: L'Abstrait c'est de la peinture mondaine, un tableau est fini quand il a effacé l'idée' in *Les Arts*, 3rd September 1953; G. JEDLICKA, 'Georges Braque' in *Universitas*, No. 9, 1954; C. AULINIER, 'La double origine du plafond de la salle Henri II au Louvre' in *Revue des Arts*, 1954; D. VALLIER, 'Georges Braque, La peinture et nous' in *Cahiers d'Art*, October 1954; J. RICHARDSON, 'The Ateliers of Braque' in *Burlington Magazine*, June 1955; J. RICHARDSON, 'Le nouvel Atelier de Braque' in *L'Oeil*, June 1955; M. VINCENT, 'Un tableau de Braque' in *Bulletin des Musées lyonnais*, No. 4, 1955; D. COOPER, *Georges Braque* (Arts Council exhibition catalogue), 1956; R. DE SOLIER, 'L'oiseau de Braque' in *Cahiers d'Art*, No. 32, 1956–7; L. GOWING, 'Two contemporaries, Braque and Ben Nicholson, in *New Statesman*, April 1957; G. LIMBOUR, 'Georges Braque, Découvertes et traditions' in *L'Oeil*, No. 33, September 1957; J. LEYMARIE, 'Georges Braque, L'Oiseau et son nid' in *Quadrum*, No. 5, 1958; J. E. CLEMENTE, 'Braque pintór del soledad' in *La Nación*, Buenos Aires, 31st August 1958; P. FRANCASTEL, *Braque e il Cubismo*, La Biennale di Venezia, August 1958; C. GREENBERG, 'Pasted Papers Revolution' in *Art News*, September 1958; J. SELZ, 'L'Oiseau et la Grève' in *Lettres nouvelles*, July 1959; J. REVOL, 'Braque et Villon, message vivant du Cubisme' in *La Nouvelle Revue Française*, August–September 1961.

SPECIAL REVIEWS

Les Soirées de Paris, 15th April 1914; *Selection*, No. 3–4, Antwerp, 1924; *Cahiers d'Art*, No. 1–2, 1933 (texts by R. Bissière, A Breton, J. Cassou, B. Cendrars, H. E. Ede, C. Einstein, A. Lhote, A. Salmon, A. Soffici, C. Zervos); *Cahiers d'Art*, 'Georges Braque', No. 12, 1937; *L'Art Sacré*, August–September 1946; *Picture Post*, 'Georges Braque: A Leader of Modern Art', 20th July 1946; *Open Og*, Amsterdam, September 1946; *L'Amour de l'Art*, 'Intimités de Braque', No. 5, 1947; *L'Art Sacré*, No. 4–5, 1947 (text by M. Florisoone); *Derrière le miroir*, June 1947 (texts by R. Char and J. Kober); *Life*, 'Georges Braque', 2nd May 1949; *Derrière le miroir*, January 1950 (texts by R. Char, A. Maldinev, J. Guignard); *Derrière le miroir*, June–July 1952 (texts by A. Giacometti and J. Grenier); *Misue*, Tokyo, October 1952 (texts by A. Imaizumi and F. Ponge); *Yomuri*, 'Georges Braque', Tokyo, 1952; *Le Point*, October 1953 (texts by S. Fumet, G. Limbour, and G. Ribemont-Dessaignes); *Verve*, No. 27–28, 1953; *Derrière le miroir*, October–November 1954 (text by G. Limbour); *France-Illustration*, 'A Varengeville avec Georges Braque', December 1954; *Verve*, 'Les carnets intimes de Georges Braque', No. 31–32, 1955 (texts by W. Grohmann, A. Tudal and R. West); *Derrière le miroir*, April–May 1956 (text by J. Lupin); *Le XXᵉ Siècle*, 'Une quête du Cubisme: le papier-collé', January 1956; *Derrière le miroir*, 1959 (text by G. Charbonnier).